YORK NOTES

D0726252

MACBETH

WILLIAM SHAKESPEARE

WORKBOOK BY MIKE GOULD

PEARSON

YORK PRESS

The right of Mike Gould to be identified as the Author of this Work has been asserted by him in accordance with the Copyright, Designs and Patents Act 1988

YORK PRESS
322 Old Brompton Road, London SW5 9JH

PEARSON EDUCATION LIMITED
Edinburgh Gate, Harlow,
Essex CM20 2JE, United Kingdom
Associated companies, branches and representatives throughout the world

First published 2015

10 9 8 7 6 5 4 3 2

ISBN 978–1–2921–0081–4

Illustrations by Sue Woollatt; and Moreno Chiacchiera (page 54 only)

Phototypeset by DTP Media
Printed in Slovakia

Photo credits: © iStock/© hidesy for page 11 top / Ilja Generalov/Shutterstock for page 12 top / RomanenkoAlexey/Shutterstock for page 15 top / cosma/Shutterstock for page 23 top / tony4urban/Shutterstock for page 25 top / Steve Byland/Shutterstock for page 29 top / Danny Smythe/Shutterstock for page 32 bottom / Sibrikov Valery/Shutterstock for page 35 top/ Kachalkina Veronika/Shutterstock for page 51 top / Stocksnapper/Shutterstock for page 52 bottom / Matt Gibson/Shutterstock for page 55 top / Michiel de Wit/Shutterstock for page 57 bottom / R Kristoffersen/Shutterstock for page 61 bottom

CONTENTS

PART ONE:
GETTING STARTED

Preparing for assessment..5

How to use your York Notes Workbook 6

PART TWO:
PLOT AND ACTION

Act I 8

Act II 16

Act III 20

Act IV 28

Act V 32

Practice task 38

PART THREE:
CHARACTERS

Who's who? 39

King Duncan 40

Macbeth 41

Lady Macbeth 42

Banquo 43

Macduff 44

The Witches 45

Malcolm, Lady Macduff and Ross............................46

Practice task...47

PART FOUR:
THEMES, CONTEXTS AND SETTINGS

Themes..48

Contexts..52

Settings...54

Practice task...56

PART FIVE:
FORM, STRUCTURE AND LANGUAGE

Form..57

Structure...58

Language...60

Practice task...63

PART SIX:
PROGRESS BOOSTER

Writing skills..64

Making inferences and interpretations................................66

Writing about context...67

Structure and linking of paragraphs 68

Spelling, punctuation and grammar....................................70

Tackling exam tasks 72

Sample answers..74

Further questions 77

Answers 78

PART ONE: Getting Started

Preparing for assessment

HOW WILL I BE ASSESSED ON MY WORK ON *MACBETH*?

All exam boards are different, but whichever course you are following, your work will be examined through these four Assessment Objectives:

Assessment Objectives	Wording	Worth thinking about ...
AO1	Read, understand and respond to texts. Students should be able to: ● maintain a critical style and develop an informed personal response ● use textual references, including quotations, to support and illustrate interpretations	● How well do I know what happens, what people say, do, etc? ● What do *I* think about the key ideas in the play? ● How can I support my viewpoint in a really convincing way? ● What are the best quotations to use and when should I use them?
AO2	Analyse the language, form and structure used by a writer to create meanings and effects, using relevant subject terminology where appropriate.	● What specific things does the writer 'do'? What choices has Shakespeare made? (Why this particular word, phrase or paragraph here? Why does this event happen at this point?) ● What effects do these choices create? Suspense? Ironic laughter? Reflective mood?
AO3	Show understanding of the relationships between texts and the contexts in which they were written.	● What can I learn about society from the play? (What does it tell me about wealth and inheritance in Shakespeare's day, for example?) ● What was society like in Shakespeare's time? Can I see it reflected in the plot?
AO4	Use a range of vocabulary and sentence structures for clarity, purpose and effect, with accurate spelling and punctuation.	● How accurately and clearly do I write? ● Are there small errors of grammar, spelling and punctuation I can get rid of?

Look out for the Assessment Objective labels throughout your York Notes Workbook – these will help to focus your study and revision!

The text used in this Workbook is the Penguin Shakespeare edition, 2005.

How to use your York Notes Workbook

There are lots of ways your Workbook can support your study and revision of *Macbeth*. There is no 'right' way – choose the one that suits your learning style best.

1) Alongside the York Notes Study Guide and the text	2) As a 'stand-alone' revision programme	3) As a form of mock-exam
Do you have the York Notes Study Guide for *Macbeth*? The contents of your Workbook are designed to match the sections in the Study Guide, so with the play to hand you could: read the relevant section(s) of the Study Guide and any part of the play referred to; complete the tasks in the same section in your Workbook.	Think you know *Macbeth* well? Why not work through the Workbook systematically, either as you finish scenes, or as you study or revise certain aspects in class or at home. You could make a revision diary and allocate particular sections of the Workbook to a day or week.	Prefer to do all your revision in one go? You could put aside a day or two and work through the Workbook, page by page. Once you have finished, check all your answers in one go! This will be quite a challenge, but it may be the approach you prefer.

HOW WILL THE WORKBOOK HELP YOU TEST AND CHECK YOUR KNOWLEDGE AND SKILLS?

Parts Two to **Five** offer a range of tasks and activities:

These fun and quick-to-complete tasks check your basic knowledge of the text

These more open questions challenge you to show your understanding

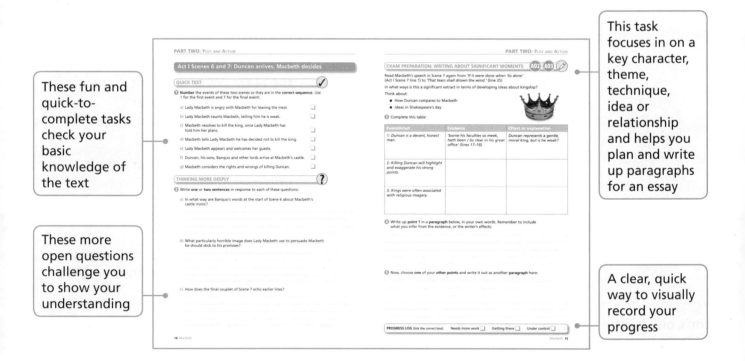

This task focuses in on a key character, theme, technique, idea or relationship and helps you plan and write up paragraphs for an essay

A clear, quick way to visually record your progress

Each Part ends with a **Practice task** to extend your revision:

An exam-style task is provided at the end of each section for you to practise a full essay

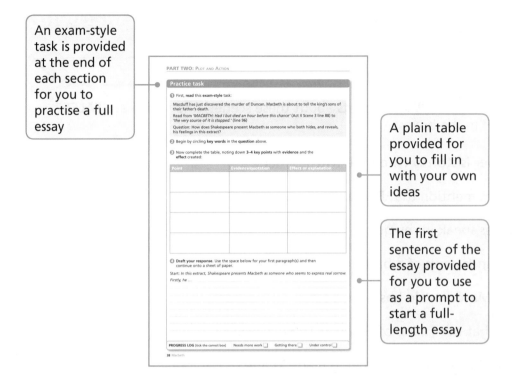

A plain table provided for you to fill in with your own ideas

The first sentence of the essay provided for you to use as a prompt to start a full-length essay

Part Six: Progress Booster helps you test your own key writing skills:

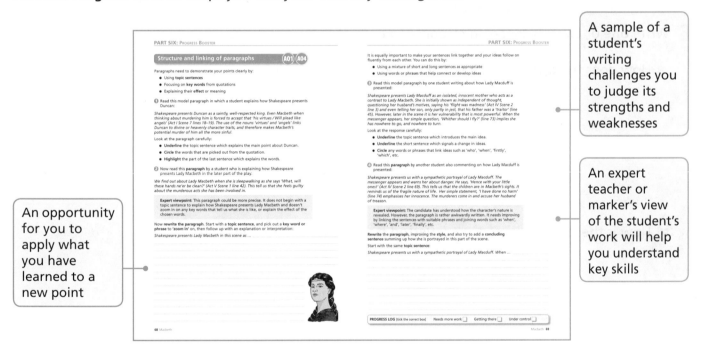

A sample of a student's writing challenges you to judge its strengths and weaknesses

An expert teacher or marker's view of the student's work will help you understand key skills

An opportunity for you to apply what you have learned to a new point

Don't forget – these are just some examples of the Workbook contents. Inside there is much, much more to help you revise. For example:

- lots of examples of students' own work at different levels
- help with spelling, punctuation and grammar
- advice and tasks on writing about context
- a full answer key so you can check your answers
- a full-length practice exam task with guidance on what to focus on.

PART TWO: PLOT AND ACTION

Act I Scenes 1 and 2: Three witches and brave Macbeth

1 Which of these are **TRUE** statements about these scenes, and which are **FALSE**? Write 'T' or 'F' in the boxes:

a) The weather is stormy when the witches meet. ☐

b) The witches mention that Banquo will arrive soon. ☐

c) The witches speak in rhyme. ☐

d) Scene 2 brings news of a battle to King Duncan. ☐

e) The rebel Macdonwald has been beaten by Macbeth. ☐

f) We learn that the Thane of Glamis is to be executed. ☐

g) Banquo will be rewarded by being made Thane of Cawdor. ☐

THINKING MORE DEEPLY **?**

2 Write **one** or **two sentences** in response to each of these questions:

a) How does the opening scene catch the audience's interest?

....

....

....

....

....

b) How is the idea of 'fair is foul' reflected by what we find out in Scene 2?

....

....

....

....

....

c) What do we learn about Banquo from the battle report in Scene 2?

....

....

....

....

....

EXAM PREPARATION: WRITING ABOUT DESCRIPTIVE LANGUAGE A02 ✎

Read from: *'But all's too weak'* (Act I Scene 2 line 15) to *'I cannot tell.'* (line 42)

Question: What picture of Macbeth does Shakespeare create from the way the Captain describes him?

Think about:

- The words used to describe Macbeth
- His actions and behaviour

③ Complete this table:

Point/detail	Evidence	Effect or explanation
1: *We learn that Macbeth is a powerful and skilful warrior.*	*'his brandished steel, / Which smoked with bloody execution'* (lines 17–18)	*His sword seemed to be on fire he used it so expertly.*
2: *He is shown to be courageous despite the danger.*		
3: *He is merciless.*		

④ Write up **point 1** in a **paragraph** below, in your own words. Remember to include what you infer from the evidence, or the writer's effects:

....
....
....
....
....
....

⑤ Now, choose **one** of your **other points** and write it out as another **paragraph** here:

....
....
....
....
....
....
....
....

PROGRESS LOG [tick the correct box]   Needs more work ☐   Getting there ☐   Under control ☐

Act I Scenes 3 and 4: Macbeth or Malcolm to be king?

QUICK TEST ✔

1 **Tick** the box for the **correct answer** to each of these questions:

a) What feature of the witches' appearance makes them unladylike, according to Banquo?

They have beards. ☐   They speak in deep voices. ☐   Their hair is cut short. ☐

b) How do the witches hail Macbeth as well as by his present title (Thane of Glamis)?

'Thane of Fife' ☐   'Thane of Cawdor' and 'King hereafter' ☐   'Thane of Forres' ☐

c) Who do the witches say will be 'Lesser than Macbeth, and greater' (Act I Scene 3 line 64)?

Duncan ☐   Malcolm ☐   Banquo ☐

d) In Scene 4, who is made heir to the throne by Duncan?

Macbeth ☐   Malcolm ☐   Macduff ☐

e) Where does Duncan tell Macbeth he is travelling to next?

Inverness ☐   Edward, the King of England's castle ☐

To watch Cawdor's execution ☐

THINKING MORE DEEPLY ❓

2 Write **one** or **two sentences** in response to each of these questions. Remember to include what you infer from the evidence, or the writer's effects:

a) Why is Macbeth surprised when Ross tells him he is the new Thane of Cawdor?

....

....

....

b) How does Banquo warn Macbeth about what the witches have promised?

....

....

....

....

c) What evidence is there at the end of Scene 4 that Macbeth is already planning Duncan's murder?

....

....

....

....

EXAM PREPARATION: WRITING ABOUT SIGNIFICANT PASSAGES

Read from *'FIRST WITCH: All hail, Macbeth! Hail to thee, Thane of Glamis!'* (Act I Scene 3 line 47) to stage direction, *'Witches vanish'* (line 77).

Question: In what ways is this passage significant?

Think about how Shakespeare presents:

* Key ideas related to prophecy and deception
* The relationship between Macbeth and Banquo

3 Complete this table:

Point/detail	Evidence	Effect or explanation
1: *Witches tell Macbeth he is Thane of Cawdor and will soon be king.*	*'be king hereafter'* (line 49)	*The promise of present and future power sows a seed in Macbeth's mind.*
2: *Language is used to develop the idea that things may not be what they seem.*		
3: *Macbeth and Banquo are shown to promise different things, suggesting they are potential rivals.*		

4 Write up **point 1** in a **paragraph** below, in your own words. Remember to include what you infer from the evidence, or the writer's effects:

....

....

....

....

....

5 Now, choose **one** of your **other points** and write it out as another **paragraph** here:

....

....

....

....

....

....

PROGRESS LOG [tick the correct box]   Needs more work ☐   Getting there ☐   Under control ☐

Act I Scene 5: Lady Macbeth's letter

QUICK TEST ✔

1 **Tick** the box for the **correct answer** to each of these questions:

a) How does Lady Macbeth find out about Macbeth's meeting with the witches and what they promised?

A servant comes to tell her ☐   She receives a letter from him ☐
Macbeth tells her himself ☐

b) What further 'tidings' are given to Lady Macbeth?

She is told the King is coming to stay ☐

Macbeth wants her to ask for a diamond from the King ☐

Banquo has been killed ☐

c) What does Lady Macbeth call on 'spirits' to do to her?

Help her sleep ☐   'Unsex' her (make her masculine) ☐   Bring her poison ☐

d) How does Lady Macbeth say Macbeth should hide his evil plans? He should…

'look like the innocent flower' ☐   dress in 'borrowed robes' ☐   be like an open 'book' ☐

THINKING MORE DEEPLY ?

2 Write **one** or **two sentences** in response to each of these questions. Remember to include what you infer from the evidence, or the writer's effects:

a) What evidence is there that Lady Macbeth and Macbeth are very close at this stage of the play?

....

....

....

....

b) How are supernatural forces reintroduced in this scene?

....

....

....

....

c) In what way does Lady Macbeth seem to be in charge of plans for Duncan at this stage?

She is already making the plans by herself.

....

....

....

....

EXAM PREPARATION: WRITING ABOUT CHARACTERISATION A02

Reread from *'LADY MACBETH: Glamis thou art'* (Act I Scene 5 line 13) to *'But be the serpent under't.'* (line 64)

Question: What do Lady Macbeth's thoughts reveal about Macbeth and her attitude to him?

Think about:

- Macbeth's willingness to do what is needed
- His ability to hide his thoughts

3 Complete this table:

Point/detail	Evidence	Effect or explanation
1: *Lady Macbeth is concerned about the more gentle side of Macbeth's nature.*	*'too full o'the milk of human-kindness' (line 15)*	*This suggests Macbeth has a womanly, nurturing side – like the one Lady Macbeth tries to get rid of in herself.*
2: *She recognises his ambition, but fears he is too passive and won't act.*		
3: *She worries that he shows his feelings too openly and needs to hide them.*		

4 Write up **point 1** in a **paragraph** below, in your own words. Remember to include what you infer from the evidence, or the writer's effects:

....
....
....
....

5 Now, choose **one** of your **other points** and write it out as another **paragraph** here:

....
....
....
....
....

PROGRESS LOG [tick the correct box] Needs more work ☐ Getting there ☐ Under control ☐

Act I Scenes 6 and 7: Duncan arrives, Macbeth decides

QUICK TEST ✓

1 **Number** the events of these two scenes so they are in the **correct sequence**. Use 1 for the first event and 7 for the final event:

a) Lady Macbeth is angry with Macbeth for leaving the meal. ☐

b) Lady Macbeth taunts Macbeth, telling him he is weak. ☐

c) Macbeth resolves to kill the king, once Lady Macbeth has told him her plans. ☐

d) Macbeth tells Lady Macbeth he has decided not to kill the king. ☐

e) Lady Macbeth appears and welcomes her guests. ☐

f) Duncan, his sons, Banquo and other lords arrive at Macbeth's castle. ☐

g) Macbeth considers the rights and wrongs of killing Duncan. ☐

THINKING MORE DEEPLY ?

2 Write **one** or **two sentences** in response to each of these questions:

a) In what way are Banquo's words at the start of Scene 6 about Macbeth's castle ironic?

....

....

....

....

b) What particularly horrible image does Lady Macbeth use to persuade Macbeth he should stick to his promises?

....

....

....

....

....

c) How does the final couplet of Scene 7 echo earlier lines?

....

....

....

....

EXAM PREPARATION: WRITING ABOUT SIGNIFICANT MOMENTS A02 A03 ✏

Read Macbeth's speech in Scene 7 again from *'If it were done when 'tis done'*
(Act I Scene 7 line 1) to *'That tears shall drown the wind.'* (line 25)

In what ways is this a significant extract in terms of developing ideas about kingship?

Think about:

- How Duncan compares to Macbeth
- Ideas in Shakespeare's day

③ Complete this table:

Point/detail	Evidence	Effect or explanation
1: *Duncan is a decent, honest man.*	*'borne his faculties so meek, hath been / So clear in his great office' (lines 17–18)*	*Duncan represents a gentle, moral king, but is he weak?*
2: *Killing Duncan will highlight and exaggerate his strong points.*		
3: *Kings were often associated with religious imagery.*		

④ Write up **point 1** in a **paragraph** below, in your own words. Remember to include what you infer from the evidence, or the writer's effects:

....

....

....

....

....

⑤ Now, choose **one** of your **other points** and write it out as another **paragraph** here:

....

....

....

....

....

....

....

PROGRESS LOG [tick the correct box]   Needs more work ☐   Getting there ☐   Under control ☐

Act II Scenes 1 and 2: Daggers and Duncan's murder

QUICK TEST ✓

1 Complete this **gap-fill paragraph** about events before and after Duncan's murder:

Scene I begins with Banquo giving Macbeth a .... to pass to Lady

Macbeth from Duncan. Macbeth is left alone and then sees an imaginary

.... which seems to be showing him the way to Duncan's

.... Despite his doubts, he presses ahead as he hears the sound of a

.... Once he has committed the murder, we find out he has foolishly

brought the ....-smeared weapons he used back with him. Lady

Macbeth is furious with him, and she takes them back so she can smear the

.... so they look as if they killed the king. She returns with blood on

her own ....

THINKING MORE DEEPLY ?

2 Write **one** or **two sentences** in response to each of these questions:

a) How does Banquo respond to Macbeth's request to support him when the time comes?

....

....

....

b) How realistic is the dagger from Macbeth's point of view?

....

....

....

....

c) What emotional state is Lady Macbeth in at the beginning of Scene 2?

....

....

....

....

EXAM PREPARATION: WRITING ABOUT WRITERS' EFFECTS

Read from *'MACBETH: Who's there? What, ho!'* (Act II Scene 2 line 8) to
'LADY MACBETH: After these ways; so, it will make us mad.' (line 34)

Question: How does Shakespeare convey the tension of the situation?

Think about:

- The style of sentences and lines
- What each character says

3 Complete this table:

Point/detail	Evidence	Effect or explanation
1: *Shakespeare's use of questions shows uncertainty.*	*'Who's there?'* (line 8) *'Did not you speak?'* (line 16)	*The questions suggest their fear of being discovered, of being heard.*
2: *Short, sometimes one-word, lines one after another show the Macbeths depending on each other.*		
3: *Macbeth is obsessed with the sleeping grooms, and what they say.*		

4 Write up **point 1** in a **paragraph** below, in your own words. Remember to include what you infer from the evidence, or the writer's effects:

....
....
....
....
....

5 Now, choose **one** of your **other points** and write it out as another **paragraph** here:

....
....
....
....
....
....
....

PROGRESS LOG [tick the correct box]   Needs more work ☐   Getting there ☐   Under control ☐

Act II Scenes 3 and 4: The murder is discovered and discussed

QUICK TEST ✓

1 Choose the **correct answer** and put a **tick** in the box:

a) Who is at the door when the Porter answers it?

Ross ☐   Macduff and Lennox ☐   Fleance ☐

b) What sort of night has it been, according to the visitors?

'Unruly' ☐   'Unreal' ☐   'Unjust' ☐

c) Who is the first person to find Duncan dead after the murder?

Lennox ☐   Macbeth ☐   Macduff ☐

d) How do Malcolm and Donalbain react?

They accuse Macbeth of murder. ☐   They faint with the shock. ☐

They decide to leave immediately. ☐

e) Where does Macduff say Macbeth has gone to be crowned king?

Colmkill ☐   Scone ☐   Fife ☐

THINKING MORE DEEPLY ?

2 Write **one** or **two sentences** in response to each of these questions:

a) What does the short section with the Porter add to the play?

....

....

....

....

b) In what way was the night disturbed, according to Lennox?

....

....

....

....

c) How do Macduff's words after the murder continue the theme of Duncan as being saintly?

....

....

....

....

EXAM PREPARATION: WRITING ABOUT A SIGNIFICANT SCENE   **A02**

Reread Act II Scene 4.

Question: What is the significance of this scene in the context of the play as a whole?

Think about:

- What we find out or are told
- The reference to certain key motifs

3 Complete this table:

Point/detail	Evidence	Effect or explanation
1: *The scene recaps what happened to the grooms; tells us that the king's sons have fled; and sows the seeds of future conflict.*	*The ones who did the deed, were 'Those that Macbeth hath slain' (line 23)* *The sons are 'stolen away' (line 26)*	*It tells us that, for now, Macbeth has 'got away with it', but the rightful heir is still alive.*
2: *Macduff is not going to Macbeth's coronation.*		
3: *The way nature has behaved reflects how the divine order has been disrupted.*		

4 Write up **point 1** in a **paragraph** below, in your own words. Remember to include what you infer from the evidence, or the writer's effects:

....

....

....

....

....

5 Now, choose **one** of your **other points** and write it out as another **paragraph** here:

....

....

....

....

....

....

....

PROGRESS LOG [tick the correct box]   Needs more work ☐   Getting there ☐   Under control ☐

Act III Scene 1: Murderous Macbeth

QUICK TEST ✔

1. **Number** the events of this scene so that they are in the **correct sequence**. Use 1 for the first event and 7 for the final event:

a) Macbeth requests Banquo's presence at his first banquet as king. ☐

b) Banquo suspects Macbeth's part in Duncan's murder. ☐

c) Macbeth asks the servant to bring in the men 'without the palace gate' (line 46). ☐

d) Macbeth asks the murderers if they have thought about his previous conversations with them. ☐

e) Banquo reveals that he and his son will go riding. ☐

f) Macbeth reflects on Banquo's character and how his heirs will be kings. ☐

g) Macbeth questions the murderers' manhood, and persuades them to kill Banquo and Fleance. ☐

THINKING MORE DEEPLY ?

2. Write **one** or **two sentences** in response to each of these questions:

a) What evidence, if any, is there that Banquo is also ambitious?

....

....

....

....

....

b) Why does Macbeth want to rid himself of Banquo?

....

....

....

....

....

c) Why does Macbeth tell the murderers he can't get rid of Banquo openly?

....

....

....

....

....

EXAM PREPARATION: WRITING ABOUT CHARACTERISATION A02

Read from *'MACBETH: Well then now'* (Act III Scene 1 lines 74–5) to *'Which in his death were perfect.'* (line 107)

Question: How does Shakespeare show that Macbeth is growing into his role as cunning villain?

Think about:

- The arguments Macbeth uses
- Macbeth's persuasive language

3 Complete this table:

Point/detail	Evidence	Effect or explanation
1: *Macbeth refers to past treatment of the men by Banquo.*	*'held you / So under fortune, which you thought had been / Our innocent self.' (lines 76–8)*	*The men were deceived into thinking it was Macbeth who hadn't promoted or helped them in life.*
2: *He questions their manhood using persuasive devices.*		
3: *There is no mention of Lady Macbeth's involvement.*		

4 Write up p**oint 1** in a **paragraph** below, in your own words. Remember to include what you infer from the evidence, or the writer's effects:

....

....

....

....

....

5 Now, choose **one** of your **other points** and write it out as another **paragraph** here:

....

....

....

....

....

....

PROGRESS LOG [tick the correct box]   Needs more work ☐   Getting there ☐   Under control ☐

Act III Scenes 2 and 3: A harder Macbeth and Banquo's death

QUICK TEST ✔

1 Which of these are **TRUE** statements about these scenes, and which are **FALSE**? Write **'T'** or **'F'** in the boxes:

a) Macbeth envies Duncan for being at peace and being able to sleep well. ☐

b) Macbeth says his mind is 'full of beetles'. ☐

c) Macbeth tells Lady Macbeth about hiring the murderers to kill Banquo. ☐

d) The second murderer thinks the reason a third has been sent to join them is because Macbeth doesn't trust them. ☐

e) The first murderer tries to help them kill Banquo by putting out the torch Banquo is carrying. ☐

f) Fleance is killed, but Banquo escapes. ☐

THINKING MORE DEEPLY ?

2 Write **one** or **two sentences** in response to each of these questions:

a) How does Macbeth's language at the end of Scene 2 link him to the powers of darkness?

....

....

....

....

....

b) What is unusual about the way the first murderer speaks near the start of Scene 3?

....

....

....

....

....

c) What is the significance of who is killed and who escapes in Scene 3?

....

....

....

....

....

EXAM PREPARATION: WRITING ABOUT LINKS WITHIN THE TEXT

Read from 'MACBETH: Let your remembrance apply to Banquo' (Act III Scene 2 line 30) to 'So, prithee, go with me.' (line 56)

Question: How does this passage both compare and contrast with Macbeth's earlier behaviour?

Think about:

- How Macbeth speaks
- What he tells Lady Macbeth

3 Complete this table:

Point/detail	Evidence	Effect or explanation
1: *Macbeth seems to be the one giving instructions.*	*'Let your remembrance apply to Banquo' (line 30)*	*Macbeth advises Lady Macbeth on how to pretend all is well with Banquo. Earlier it was the other way around.*
2: *Macbeth's last speech is similar to Lady Macbeth's in Act I Scene 5, showing his cold-blooded nature.*		
3: *He doesn't share his plans for Banquo with his wife.*		

4 Write up **point 1** into a **paragraph** below in your own words. Remember to include what you infer from the evidence, or the writer's effects:

....

....

....

....

5 Now, choose **one** of your **other points** and write it out as another **paragraph** here:

....

....

....

....

....

PROGRESS LOG [tick the correct box]   Needs more work ☐   Getting there ☐   Under control ☐

Act III Scene 4: Banquo's ghost

QUICK TEST ✓

1 **Tick** the box with the **correct answer** to each of these questions:

a) Who says he cut Banquo's throat?

Ross ☐   First murderer ☐   Second murderer ☐

b) Who is able to see Banquo's ghost?

Macbeth ☐   Macbeth and Lady Macbeth ☐   Everyone at the banquet ☐

c) How does Lady Macbeth try to explain Macbeth's behaviour to the guests?

She tells them he feels guilty. ☐   She says it's a childhood illness. ☐

She says he has poor eyesight. ☐

d) Who has refused to come to see Macbeth?

Macduff ☐   Malcolm ☐   Menteth ☐

e) How does Macbeth know what his enemies are thinking?

The witches have told him. ☐   He has had dreams at night. ☐

He has a paid spy in each of their houses. ☐

THINKING MORE DEEPLY ?

2 Write **one** or **two sentences** in response to each of these questions:

a) In what way should this be the high point for the Macbeths?

....

....

....

....

b) How does Lady Macbeth taunt Macbeth over his behaviour?

....

....

....

....

c) Why does Macbeth decide to continue with his murderous plans despite the effect it has had on him?

....

....

....

....

EXAM PREPARATION: WRITING ABOUT PRESENTATION OF THEMES (A02)

Read from *'MACBETH: The table's full.'* (Act III Scene 4 line 45) to *'Unreal mockery, hence!'* (line 106)

Question: How is the theme of the supernatural developed in this extract?

Think about:

- What the supernatural reveals
- How this links with other uses of the supernatural in the play

3 Complete this table:

Point/detail	Evidence	Effect or explanation
1: *This is the first of the visions related to Banquo and kingship.*	*'Here is a place reserved, sir.'* (line 45)	*Banquo's ghost sits in Macbeth's place, reminding us that his children will ultimately inherit the throne, something we see enacted again in Act IV Scene 1.*
2: *Visions related to the murder are seen only by Macbeth.*		
3: *The supernatural has the capacity to violently disturb as well as to encourage.*		

4 Write up **point 1** into a **paragraph** below in your own words. Remember to include what you infer from the evidence, or the writer's effects:

....

....

....

....

....

5 Now, choose **one** of your **other points** and write it out as another **paragraph** here:

....

....

....

....

....

....

PROGRESS LOG [tick the correct box]   Needs more work ☐   Getting there ☐   Under control ☐

Act III Scenes 5 and 6: Hecat's plans and Lennox's report

QUICK TEST ✓

1 Which of these are **TRUE** statements about what we find out from these scenes, and which are **FALSE**? Write **'T'** or **'F'** in the boxes:

a) Hecat is delighted with the three witches. ☐

b) Hecat predicts Macbeth's downfall from over-confidence. ☐

c) Lennox genuinely believes Fleance killed his own father. ☐

d) Malcolm is living in England in Edward's court. ☐

e) Macduff has gone to raise an army in Northumberland. ☐

f) Macduff finally agrees to return when Macbeth sends a message to him. ☐

THINKING MORE DEEPLY ?

2 Write **one** or **two sentences** in response to each of these questions:

a) Why do you think some productions leave out Scene 5 altogether?

....
....
....
....

b) What does the use of the word 'tyrant' (Act III Scene 6 lines 22 and 25) tell us about the changing view of Macbeth at this stage of the play?

....
....
....
....

c) How does the Lord's long speech in Scene 6 advance the plot?

....
....
....
....
....

EXAM PREPARATION: WRITING ABOUT EFFECTS   A02

Read Lennox's long speech at the start of Act III Scene 6.

Question: How does Shakespeare convey Lennox's viewpoint on the state of affairs in Scotland?

Think about:

● The particular hints and clues he gives

● The tone of his language

3 Complete this table:

Point/detail	Evidence	Effect or explanation
1: *Lennox uses guarded language to express doubts about Banquo's murder.*	*'Whom you may say, if't please you, Fleance killed, / For Fleance fled.' (lines 6–7)*	*The phrase 'if't please you' suggests that this is not based on reality but what Macbeth would like you to think.*
2: *He uses irony to criticise Macbeth about killing the servants.*		
3: *He hints that he is pleased Duncan's sons have not been captured by Macbeth.*		

4 Write up **point 1** into a **paragraph** below in your own words. Remember to include what you infer from the evidence, or the writer's effects:

....

....

....

....

....

5 Now, choose **one** of your **other points** and write it out as another **paragraph** here:

....

....

....

....

....

....

....

PROGRESS LOG [tick the correct box]   Needs more work ☐   Getting there ☐   Under control ☐

Act IV Scenes 1 and 2: Prophecies, and murder of the Macduffs

QUICK TEST ✔

1 **Tick** the box with the **correct answer** to each of these questions:

a) How does Act IV Scene 1 begin?

With the witches' spells ☐   With visions of the future ☐

With Macbeth on horseback ☐

b) Who do the witches say can't harm Macbeth?

'The Thane of Fife' ☐   'Fleance' ☐   'None of woman born' ☐

c) How many kings are 'shown' to Macbeth by the witches?

Three ☐   Eight ☐   Ten ☐

d) Which Lord is with Lady Macduff as Scene 2 opens?

Ross ☐   Angus ☐   Seyward ☐

e) What does the murderer call Macduff?

A villain ☐   An egg ☐   A traitor ☐

THINKING MORE DEEPLY ?

2 Write **one** or **two sentences** in response to each of these questions:

a) What particular destructive actions does Macbeth say the witches are capable of in Act IV Scene 1?

....

....

....

....

b) What evidence is there that Macbeth does not entirely trust the prophecies?

....

....

....

....

c) What evidence is there that Macbeth is unnerved by the apparition of the kings and Banquo?

....

....

....

....

EXAM PREPARATION: WRITING ABOUT EFFECTS A02 A03

Read from *'MACDUFF'S WIFE: Wisdom! To leave his wife'* (Act IV Scene 2 line 6) to *'SON: Poor birds they are not set for.'* (line 37)

Question: How does the use of figurative language add to the drama and emotion of the scene?

Think about:

- How a father's duty is described
- What we know is going to happen

3 Complete this table:

Point/detail	Evidence	Effect or explanation
1: *Lady Macduff suggests that her husband has abandoned them – which has some truth in it.*	*'for the poor wren ... will fight ... against the owl.' (lines 9–11)*	*This analogy, which links Lady Macduff and her children to tiny birds who stand up to a cruel predator, makes us sympathise with her plight.*
2: *Ross describes the current state of the world and how difficult it is to survive.*		
3: *Lady Macduff's son says he isn't afraid.*		

4 Write up **point 1** into a **paragraph** below in your own words. Remember to include what you infer from the evidence, or the writer's effects:

....
....
....
....
....

5 Now, choose **one** of your **other points** and write it out as another **paragraph** here:

....
....
....
....
....

PROGRESS LOG [tick the correct box]   Needs more work ☐   Getting there ☐   Under control ☐

Act IV Scene 3: Malcolm and Macduff

QUICK TEST ✓

1 **Number** the events of this scene so that they are in the **correct sequence**. Use 1 for the first event and 7 for the final event:

a) Doctor and Malcolm comment on King Edward's saintliness. ☐

b) Macduff prepares to leave, believing Malcolm's words about himself. ☐

c) Malcolm questions why Macduff left his family so suddenly. ☐

d) Malcolm reveals he was testing Macduff's loyalty. ☐

e) Malcolm says if he were king he would be even more greedy and violent than Macbeth. ☐

f) Malcolm and Macduff resolve to remove Macbeth as king. ☐

g) Ross brings news that Macduff's family have been murdered. ☐

THINKING MORE DEEPLY ?

2 Write **one** or **two sentences** in response to each of these questions:

a) Why did Malcolm feel the need to test Macduff's loyalty?

....
....
....
....

b) In what way does Ross both reveal and hide the truth about Macduff's family's death to begin with?

....
....
....
....

c) What comparisons to animals are made by Ross and Macduff to stress the cruelty of the murder?

....
....
....
....
....

EXAM PREPARATION: WRITING ABOUT KEY THEMES

Read from *'MALCOLM: Macduff, this noble passion'* (Act IV Scene 3 line 114) to *'speak him full of grace.'* (line 159)

Question: How does this section further develop the theme of kingship?

Think about:

● Malcolm's description of himself

● The descriptions of Edward and Macbeth

❸ Complete this table:

Point/detail	Evidence	Effect or explanation
1: *Malcolm's description of himself creates a contrast with Macbeth's cruelty.*	*'My first false speaking / Was this upon myself.'* *(lines 130–1)*	*Malcolm's pretending to be evil is the first time he's been dishonest – Macbeth's 'false-speaking' has been shown many times.*
2: *Edward's healing ability underlines the divine right of kings.*		
3: *Edward's saintliness reminds us of Duncan.*		

❹ Write up **point 1** into a **paragraph** below in your own words. Remember to include what you infer from the evidence, or the writer's effects:

....

....

....

....

....

❺ Now, choose **one** of your **other points** and write it out as another **paragraph** here:

....

....

....

....

....

....

PROGRESS LOG [tick the correct box]   Needs more work ☐   Getting there ☐   Under control ☐

Act V Scene 1: Lady Macbeth's sleepwalking

QUICK TEST ✔

1 Which of these are **TRUE** statements about this scene, and which are **FALSE**? Write 'T' or 'F' in the boxes:

a) This is the first night the Doctor has spent time watching Lady Macbeth. ☐

b) The Gentlewoman refuses to reveal what Lady Macbeth has said previously while sleepwalking. ☐

c) The first sight of Lady Macbeth is of her carrying a candle. ☐

d) Her first words are, 'Yet another stain on my hand.' ☐

e) Lady Macbeth tries to clean her hands while sleepwalking. ☐

f) Lady Macbeth refers to three murders in her speech. ☐

g) After she has sleepwalked, she wakes up and talks normally to the Doctor. ☐

THINKING MORE DEEPLY ?

2 Write **one** or **two sentences** in response to each of these questions:

a) Why does Shakespeare choose to put this scene in prose rather than blank verse?

....

....

....

....

b) In what way is Lady Macbeth's reference to not being able to remove blood ironic given her earlier statements?

....

....

....

....

c) What sort of help does the Doctor think she needs, and why?

....

....

....

....

....

....

EXAM PREPARATION: WRITING ABOUT THE THEME OF GUILT

Read from *'DOCTOR: What is it she does now?'* (Act V Scene 1 line 26) to *'LADY MACBETH: To bed, to bed, to bed.'* (line 64)

Question: Why is this scene significant in developing the theme of guilt?

Think about:

- What Lady Macbeth says and does
- What you know of her before this scene

3 Complete this table:

Point/detail	Evidence	Effect or explanation
1: *Lady Macbeth's earlier comments about Duncan looking like her father affected her more than we thought.*	*'Yet who would have thought the old man to have had so much blood in him?' (lines 38–9)*	*Lady Macbeth is fixated on and horrified by the amount of blood that has been spilt.*
2: *Shakespeare suggests that guilt cannot be easily removed.*		
3: *Her words ironically echo her earlier arguments to persuade Macbeth in Act II Scene 2.*		

4 Write up **point 1** into a **paragraph** below in your own words. Remember to include what you infer from the evidence, or the writer's effects:

....

....

....

....

....

5 Now, choose **one** of your **other points** and write it out as another **paragraph** here:

....

....

....

....

....

....

PROGRESS LOG [tick the correct box]   Needs more work ☐   Getting there ☐   Under control ☐

Act V Scenes 2 and 3: The rebels and Macbeth prepare

QUICK TEST ✔

1 Tick the box with the **correct answer** to each of these questions:

a) Which of the aristocratic sons is missing from the English/Scottish army?

Malcolm ☐   Seyward's son ☐   Donalbain ☐

b) Angus describes Macbeth's crown/rule being like 'a giant's robe on a …'

'dwarfish thief' ☐   'thoughtful dwarf' ☐   'drunken thane' ☐

c) How many soldiers does Macbeth face, according to the servant?

1,000 ☐   10,000 ☐   100,000 ☐

d) What does Macbeth say his life is withered like?

'Rooted sorrow' ☐   'Perilous stuff' ☐   'The yellow leaf' ☐

e) Who, according to Seyton, is 'troubled with thick-coming fancies' (Act V Scene 3 line 38)?

Lady Macbeth ☐   Macbeth ☐   Macduff ☐

THINKING MORE DEEPLY ?

2 Write **one** or **two sentences** in response to each of these questions:

a) According to Angus, how well-supported is Macbeth in his rule?

b) What impression do we get of how Macbeth feels about the coming battle?

c) How does Macbeth treat the servant when he brings reports of the numbers facing Macbeth?

EXAM PREPARATION: WRITING ABOUT DEVELOPING AN IDEA

Read from *'MENTETH: What does the tyrant?'* (Act V Scene 2 line 11) to *'LENNOX: Make we our march towards Birnan.'* (line 31)

Question: How does Shakespeare draw on ideas about disease and illness to describe Macbeth's rule?

Think about:

- How Scotland and Macbeth's rule is described
- The role of Malcolm/Seyward's army

3 Complete this table:

Point/detail	Evidence	Effect or explanation
1: *Macbeth's rule is seen as a disease.*	*'cannot buckle his distempered cause / Within the belt of rule.'* (lines 15–16)	*Macbeth's cause is evil, so he himself has lost control, like an illness that can't be kept in.*
2: *The invading army is seen as the necessary cure to get rid of the disease (Macbeth).*		
3: *Macbeth is compared to a destructive weed that needs killing off.*		

4 Write up **point 1** into a **paragraph** below in your own words. Remember to include what you infer from the evidence, or the writer's effects:

....

....

....

....

....

5 Now, choose **one** of your **other points** and write it out as another **paragraph** here:

....

....

....

....

....

PROGRESS LOG [tick the correct box]   Needs more work ☐   Getting there ☐   Under control ☐

Act V Scenes 4, 5 and 6: Defeat, death and prophecies revealed

QUICK TEST ✔

1 **Number** the events of these scenes so that they are in the **correct sequence**. Use 1 for the first event and 7 for the final event:

a) A messenger tells Macbeth that he has seen Birnan Wood move. ☐

b) Malcolm orders his army to camouflage themselves using trees from Birnan Wood. ☐

c) Macbeth kills Young Seyward in a fight. ☐

d) Seyton informs Macbeth that Lady Macbeth is dead. ☐

e) Macduff tells Macbeth of his unusual birth, 'untimely ripped' (Scene 6 line 55) from his mother. ☐

f) Malcolm is hailed as king and invites everyone to see him crowned at Scone. ☐

g) Macbeth is killed by Macduff. ☐

THINKING MORE DEEPLY ?

2 Write **one** or **two sentences** in response to each of these questions:

a) How do the final scenes satisfy our curiosity about the prophecies?

....

....

....

....

b) In what ways are we reminded of Macbeth's original qualities in these scenes?

....

....

....

....

c) Why does Shakespeare include the detail of Young Seyward being killed by Macbeth?

....

....

....

....

....

EXAM PREPARATION: WRITING ABOUT EFFECTS   A02

Reread Act V scenes 4, 5 and 6.

Question: How does Shakespeare create dramatic impact in the final three scenes?

Think about:

- What happens
- How it is described

3 Complete this table:

Point/detail	Evidence	Effect or explanation
1: *We witness the one-to-one combat between Macbeth and Macduff.*	*'Turn, hellhound, turn!' (Act V Scene 6 line 42)*	*This satisfies our desire to see Macbeth meet his fate and for good to triumph.*
2: *Shakespeare cleverly reveals how the prophecies have come true, and have 'tricked' Macbeth.*		
3: *Shakespeare introduces movement and action which in turn creates excitement.*		

4 Write up **point 1** into a **paragraph** below in your own words. Remember to include what you infer from the evidence, or the writer's effects:

....

....

....

....

5 Now, choose **one** of your **other points** and write it out as another **paragraph** here:

....

....

....

....

....

....

PROGRESS LOG [tick the correct box]   Needs more work ☐   Getting there ☐   Under control ☐

Practice task

1 First, **read** this **exam-style** task:

Macduff has just discovered the murder of Duncan. Macbeth is about to tell the king's sons of their father's death.

Read from *'MACBETH: Had I but died an hour before this chance'* (Act II Scene 3 line 88) to *'the very source of it is stopped.'* (line 96)

Question: How does Shakespeare present Macbeth as someone who both hides, and reveals, his feelings in this extract?

2 Begin by circling **key words** in the **question** above.

3 Now complete the table, noting down **3–4 key points** with **evidence** and the **effect** created:

Point	Evidence/quotation	Effect or explanation

4 **Draft your response**. Use the space below for your first paragraph(s) and then continue onto a sheet of paper.

Start: *In this extract, Shakespeare presents Macbeth as someone who seems to express real sorrow.*

Firstly, he … ....

....

....

....

....

....

....

....

PROGRESS LOG [tick the correct box]   Needs more work ☐   Getting there ☐   Under control ☐

PART THREE: CHARACTERS

Who's who?

1 Look at these drawings and **add** the **missing information** for each of the characters shown, without checking the play or your own study guide.

Name: ....

Who: *Friend of Macbeth*

Name: ....

Who: *Thane of Glamis (at start)*

Name: ....

Who: *Queen of Scotland (for a time)*

Name: ....

Who: ....

Name: ....

Who: *Thane of Fife*

Names: *unknown*

Who: ....

Name: *Malcolm*

Who: ....

Name: ....

Who: *Earl of Northumberland*

2 Which **characters** are **missing** from the section above? Fill in the table below:

Scottish lords or ladies	Scottish children: other sons, daughters, brothers, or sisters	Characters from England who fight against Macbeth	Others?

King Duncan

1 Look at these statements about Duncan and decide whether they are **True [T]**,
False [F] or whether there is **Not Enough Evidence [NEE]**.

a) Duncan is king of Scotland.   [T] [F] [NEE]

b) He trusted the traitorous Thane of Cawdor.   [T] [F] [NEE]

c) Duncan shows his respect for Lady Macbeth by giving
   her a diamond.   [T] [F] [NEE]

d) Duncan rewards Banquo by making him Thane of Fife.   [T] [F] [NEE]

e) Duncan is regarded as a weak king.   [T] [F] [NEE]

f) Malcolm is Duncan's only son.   [T] [F] [NEE]

g) Duncan is killed while asleep at Macbeth's castle.   [T] [F] [NEE]

2 **Complete** these **statements** about Duncan:

a) *Duncan's kingdom is under threat at the start of the play from ...* ....

....

....

....

b) *Duncan shows himself to be a poor judge of character by ...* ....

....

....

....

c) *Macbeth is reluctant to kill Duncan because ...* ....

....

....

d) *Although Duncan is killed early in the play, he casts a shadow over Macbeth*
   because ... .

....

....

....

....

e) *Duncan is linked to other characters in the play, such as ...* ....

....

....

PROGRESS LOG [tick the correct box]   Needs more work ☐   Getting there ☐   Under control ☐

Macbeth

1 Without looking at the play, **write down from memory** at least two pieces of information we are told about Macbeth in each of these areas:

Macbeth's abilities as a soldier and warrior	1 2
His changing feelings of conscience	1 2
His murderous acts	1 2

Now **check your ideas**. Are you right? Look at the following scenes from the play:

- Macbeth's abilities as a soldier and warrior: Act I Scene 2, Act V Scenes 3–6
- His changing feelings of conscience: Act I Scene 7, Act II Scenes 1 and 2, Act III Scene 4, Act IV Scene 1
- His murders: Act II Scene 3, Act III Scene 1, Act IV Scene 2

2 Do you think Macbeth is more ambitious for power than Lady Macbeth? Sort the evidence below into **'For'** and **'Against'** by ticking the appropriate column. Think carefully – some evidence could prove either viewpoint.

Evidence	For	Against
Macbeth immediately thinks about how he can overcome the fact that Malcolm is made heir.		
Lady Macbeth makes the plans for Duncan's murder.		
Macbeth seems guilty and reluctant to kill the king.		
Lady Macbeth has to persuade him to go through with it.		
He carries out the killing himself, and kills the servants.		
He organises the murders of Banquo and Macduff's family.		

PROGRESS LOG [tick the correct box]   Needs more work ☐   Getting there ☐   Under control ☐

Lady Macbeth

1 Look at this bank of **adjectives** describing Lady Macbeth. Circle the ones you think best **describe** her:

> *murderous   evil   ambitious   proud   feminine   motherly   cruel*
>
> *dignified   unstable   gentle   welcoming   cunning   desperate*
>
> *powerful   violent   guilty*

2 Complete this **gap-fill paragraph** about Lady Macbeth, adding the **correct information**:

We first meet Lady Macbeth as she is reading a letter from .... in

Act I Scene 5, which seems to sow the seeds for ....'s murder.

However, she is concerned about whether Macbeth has the .... to

carry out the plans and she has to question his .... in

order to get him to act. When Macbeth falters both after the murder of the

king, and at the banquet, she has to invent .... for his

behaviour. But, increasingly, he acts without consulting her, preferring her to

be '............................ of the knowledge' (Act III Scene 2 line 45). The stress of

maintaining their position and the thought of the murders of Duncan, Banquo

and Lady .... clearly weigh on her mind, and she suffers terrible

.... Eventually, we find out that she has died 'by self and violent

hands' (Act V Scene 6 line 109), according to Malcolm who calls her a

'...............-like queen' (Act V Scene 6 line 108).

3 Using your **own judgement**, put a mark along this line to show **Shakespeare's overall presentation** of Lady Macbeth:

Totally unsympathetic	A little sympathetic	Quite sympathetic	Very sympathetic
①	②	③	④

PROGRESS LOG [tick the correct box]   Needs more work ☐   Getting there ☐   Under control ☐

Banquo

1 **Complete** these **quotations** either by Banquo, or describing him:

a) First Witch: '............................ than Macbeth, and greater.'
(Act I Scene 3 line 64)

b) Duncan: '............................ Banquo, / That hast no less deserved'
(Act I Scene 4 lines 30–1)

c) 'I fear / thou playedst most .... for't (Act III Scene1 lines 2–3)

d) Macbeth: 'There is none but he / Whose being I do ....'
(Act III Scene 1 lines 54–5)

e) 'I drink to the general joy o'the whole table, / And to our
.... Banquo, whom we miss.' (Act III Scene 4 lines 88–9)

2 Put the **letters** for each of these points about Banquo on the **suitable side** of the weighing scales to show how ambitious you think he is:

....
....
....
....

ambitious   not ambitious

....
....
....

a) He asks the witches about his future in Act I Scene 3.

b) He bravely fights alongside Macbeth in battle for Duncan.

c) He isn't given any special reward other than thanks by Duncan.

d) He thinks about the prophecies at the start of Act III Scene 1.

e) Macbeth says he is the only person that makes him afraid.

f) He dreams of the witches the night before Duncan's murder.

g) He refuses to commit to supporting Macbeth.

h) He is desperate for Fleance to escape the murderers.

3 **Write a paragraph** explaining **how Shakespeare presents Banquo**. Try to use some of the information above, including at least one quotation:

I think Shakespeare wants to present Banquo as ... .
....
....
....

PROGRESS LOG [tick the correct box]   Needs more work ☐   Getting there ☐   Under control ☐

Macduff

1 Who says? Circle the name of the character who makes these **statements** about, or to, Macduff?

a) 'Who's there i' the name of Belzebub?' (Act II Scene3 lines 3–4)

The Porter ☐   Ross ☐   Third witch ☐

b) 'Macduff denies his person / At our great bidding?' (Act III Scene 4 lines 127–8)

Macbeth ☐   Lady Macbeth ☐   Lady Macduff ☐

c) 'I hear / Macduff lives in disgrace.' (Act III Scene 6 22–3)

Angus ☐   Lennox ☐   Ross ☐

d) 'He loves us not. / He wants the natural touch' (Act IV Scene 2 lines 8–9)

Malcolm ☐   Macduff's son ☐   Lady Macduff ☐

e) 'Give sorrow words: the grief that does not speak / Whispers the o'erfraught heart and bids it break.' (Act IV Scene 3 lines 209–10)

Malcolm ☐   Doctor ☐   Duncan ☐

f) 'my soul is too much charged / With blood of thine already.' (Act V Scene 6 lines 44–5)

Third murderer ☐   Macbeth ☐   Lady Macbeth ☐

2 Write **two sentences** in response to each of these questions:

a) Why did Macbeth give the order to slaughter Macduff and his family?

b) What seem to be Macduff's reasons for leaving his family to go to England?

c) What is his reaction on hearing that his whole family has been murdered?

PROGRESS LOG [tick the correct box]   Needs more work ☐   Getting there ☐   Under control ☐

The witches

1 Look at these statements about the witches and decide whether they are **True [T]**, **False [F]** or for which there is **Not Enough Evidence [NEE]**.

a) The witches mention Macbeth before we see him on the stage.   [T] [F] [NEE]

b) The witches are seen only by Macbeth.   [T] [F] [NEE]

c) They are really ordinary women, not spirits or phantoms.   [T] [F] [NEE]

d) Their brew in Act IV Scene 1 includes a dragon's scales.   [T] [F] [NEE]

e) The witches tell Macbeth directly to 'beware the Thane of Fife'.   [T] [F] [NEE]

2 **Complete these statements** about the witches:

a) *The witches' opening scene establishes some important themes in the play such as …* ....

....

....

b) *The witches' prophecies for Banquo have a riddling quality because …* ....

....

....

c) *In Act IV Scene 1, Macbeth believes that the witches have the power to affect the natural world, for example …* ....

....

....

3 **Write a paragraph** explaining the significance of the witches to the play as a whole:

I think the witches are significant to the play because they … ....

....

....

....

....

....

....

....

....

....

....

PROGRESS LOG [tick the correct box]   Needs more work ☐   Getting there ☐   Under control ☐

Malcolm, Lady Macduff and Ross

1 **Who says?** Tick the character who speaks each line.

Quotation	Malcolm	Lady Macduff	Ross
'This murderous shaft that's shot / Hath not yet lighted' (Act II Scene 3 lines 138–9)			
'By the clock 'tis day, / And yet dark night strangles the travelling lamp' (Act II Scene 4 lines 6–7)			
'I take my leave of you; / Shall not be long but I'll be here again.' (Act IV Scene 2 lines 22–3)			
'I have done no harm.' (Act IV Scene 2 line 74)			
'Macbeth / Is ripe for shaking.' (Act IV Scene 3 lines 236–7)			

2 Write at least **one sentence** in response to these questions:

a) Why does Malcolm flee with his brother after their father's death?

....

....

b) What news does Ross bring Macbeth at the start of the play?

....

....

c) Why is Lady Macduff confused and upset at the start of Act IV Scene 2?

....

....

3 **Complete these statements** about each character, using your own judgement:

a) *I believe that Shakespeare presents Malcolm as a <u>good/bad</u> king of the future because ...* ....

....

b) *In my opinion, Shakespeare presents Ross as <u>trustworthy/untrustworthy</u> because ...* ....

....

c) *In my opinion Lady Macduff is <u>important/not that important</u> to the play because ...* ....

....

PROGRESS LOG [tick the correct box]   Needs more work ☐   Getting there ☐   Under control ☐

Practice task

1 First, **read** this **exam-style** task:

Read the extract in Act I Scene 5 from *'MACBETH: My dearest love'* (line 56) to *'LADY MACBETH: Leave all the rest to me.'* (line 71).

Question: How does Shakespeare present Lady Macbeth as a powerful woman?

Think about:
- This extract
- The play as a whole

2 Begin by circling the **key words** in the **question** above.

3 Now complete the table, noting down **3–4 key points** with **evidence** and the **effect** created:

Point	Evidence/quotation	Effect or explanation

4 **Draft your response.** Use the space below for your first paragraph(s) and then continue onto a sheet of paper.

Start: *In this extract, Shakespeare presents Lady Macbeth as someone who is clearly taking a leading role in making plans. Firstly …*

....

....

....

....

....

....

....

PROGRESS LOG [tick the correct box]   Needs more work ☐   Getting there ☐   Under control ☐

PART FOUR: THEMES, CONTEXTS AND SETTINGS

Themes

1 **Circle** the **themes** you think are most relevant to *Macbeth*:

ambition	witchcraft	the supernatural	fate	revenge	kingship
guilt	motherhood	fatherhood	conflict	regret	betrayal	love
greed	evil	religion	journeys	childhood	appearance versus reality

2 **Who says?** Each of these quotations relates to a theme, but which one (or more), and who is speaking?

a) 'Peace! The charm's wound up.' (Act I Scene 3 line 36)

Theme(s): .... Speaker(s): ....

b) 'Your children shall be kings.' (Act I Scene 3 line 85)

Theme(s): .... Speaker(s): ....

c) 'Come, thick night / And pall thee in the dunnest smoke of hell'
(Act I Scene 5 lines 48–9)

Theme(s): .... Speaker(s): ....

d) 'art thou but / A dagger of the mind, a false creation, / Proceeding from the
heat-oppressèd brain?' (Act II Scene 1 lines 37–9)

Theme(s): .... Speaker(s): ....

e) 'Front to front / Bring thou this fiend of Scotland and myself. / Within my
sword's length set him' (Act IV Scene 3 lines 231–3)

Theme(s): .... Speaker(s): ....

f) 'Of all men else I have avoided thee. /... my soul is too much charged / With
blood of thine already.' (Act V Scene 6, 43–5)

Theme(s): .... Speaker(s): ....

PROGRESS LOG [tick the correct box]   Needs more work ☐   Getting there ☐   Under control ☐

THINKING MORE DEEPLY

3 Think about the **themes** of the **supernatural** and **witchcraft**. Write **one or two sentences** in response to each of these questions:

a) Why do you think Shakespeare opened the play with the short witches' scene?

....

....

....

....

b) At what point in the play does Lady Macbeth seem to be calling on evil spirits to give her the strength to carry out terrible crimes?

....

....

....

....

4 **Visions** are an important element in the play. Can you think of **three occasions** when characters see things that are so powerful they seem real (other than in the scenes with the witches)?

a) ....

b) ....

c) ....

5 **Write down** how each of these **prophecies** happens, or is seen to be true:

a) Macbeth is told he is Thane of Cawdor, yet he is in fact Thane of Glamis.

Comes true because: ....

....

....

b) Macbeth is told he is safe until Birnan Wood moves to Dunsinane (his castle).

Comes true because: ....

....

....

c) Macbeth is told he cannot be harmed by anyone 'of woman born' (Act IV Scene 1 line 79).

Comes true because: ....

....

....

PROGRESS LOG [tick the correct box]   Needs more work ☐   Getting there ☐   Under control ☐

6 Complete this **gap-fill paragraph** about the **theme** of **betrayal**:

We find out early in the play that the Thane of .... has betrayed

Duncan. Duncan admits that he finds it difficult to 'find the ....

construction in the face', in other words to read people's thoughts. Both Lady

Macbeth and Macbeth betray Duncan by welcoming him to ....

and pretending to be kind hosts, and then murdering him. But the betrayal is also

of the innocent .... who are also killed. Macbeth might feel that

.... betrays him when he refuses to commit to supporting him, but

the real betrayal is when Macbeth orders the murders of Banquo and his son,

.... Perhaps the biggest betrayal in the play is not of one person,

but of a country – .... It is said that it '....................' and 'bleeds'

(Act IV Scene 3 line 40) under Macbeth's rule.

7 **Think** about the **theme** of **kingship**.

a) Using your **own judgement**, rate these kings from **1 (low)** to **(5) high** in each of
these areas, then give a total out of 15:

	bravery	judgement	goodness	Total
Duncan				
Macbeth				
Edward (King of England)				
Malcolm				

b) Now write **one or two sentences** saying **who** you think makes the best king
and **why**:

....

....

....

....

....

....

....

EXAM PREPARATION: WRITING ABOUT THE SUPERNATURAL

Reread the section from *'MACBETH (aside): Glamis, and Thane of Cawdor! The greatest is behind.'* (Act I Scene 3 lines 115–16) to *'BANQUO: ... In deepest consequence.'* (line 125)

Question: Starting with this conversation, explore how Shakespeare presents attitudes towards the supernatural in *Macbeth*.

Think about:

- What Macbeth and Banquo have to say about the witches' promises
- How the supernatural is presented in the rest of the play

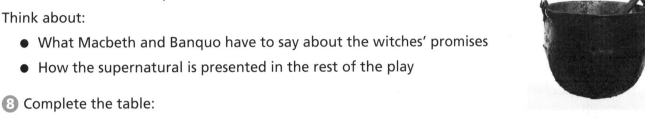

8 Complete the table:

Point/detail	Evidence	Effect or explanation
1: *Macbeth sees his own future success in what the witches have said.*	*Macbeth: 'The greatest is behind' (line 116)*	*The witches have proved correct on one promise, so the next step is now in sight.*
2: *Banquo is less trusting of the witches.*		
3: *The supernatural can be frightening and both hide and reveal the truth.*		

9 Write up **point 1** into a **paragraph** below in your own words. Remember to include what you infer from the evidence, or the writer's effects:

....

....

....

....

....

10 Now, choose **one** of your **other points** and write it out as another **paragraph** here:

....

....

....

....

....

....

....

PROGRESS LOG [tick the correct box]   Needs more work ☐   Getting there ☐   Under control ☐

Contexts

QUICK TEST

1️⃣ **Choose** the **correct answer** to these questions:

a) Which historical writer did Shakespeare use to get his information about Macbeth (a real person)?

Holinshed ☐   The Venerable Bede ☐   Chaucer ☐

b) The play *Macbeth* has been performed in many different versions. One was a gangster film. What was it called?

The Scotfather ☐   *Joe Macbeth* ☐   *Macbeth, King of the Mafia* ☐

c) Who was King of England (and Scotland) when the play *Macbeth* was first performed?

Elizabeth I ☐   James I ☐   James II ☐

d) What was the name of the book written by the King about witches and similar matters?

The Discovery of Witches ☐   *Malleus maleficarum* ☐   *Demonology* ☐

e) What famous historical event might the Porter be referring to in his speech?

The appearance of Halley's comet ☐   The Gunpowder Plot ☐
The defeat of the Spanish Armada ☐

f) Why might Shakespeare have written plays that appealed to the King?

The King was Shakespeare's patron ☐   It was the law ☐
The King checked every script ☐

g) The play focuses on the question of who will become king after Duncan. What is the proper term that historians use for this?

The inheritance ☐   The recession ☐   The succession ☐

h) Medieval kings wanted to believe that they had been chosen by God. What is the term for this?

Divine Right of Kings ☐   Eternal Law of God ☐   True Path of Heaven ☐

THINKING MORE DEEPLY

2 Write **one or two sentences** in answer to each of these questions:

a) There was a great deal of uncertainty in Shakespeare's time about who should be king, and war and rebellion were a constant problem. How is this shown in the opening two scenes of the play?

....

....

....

b) How is the rightful order (in terms of ruling Scotland) put back into place at the end of the play?

....

....

....

c) Shakespeare chose to make some changes from the historical sources he used. For example, in reality Banquo probably helped murder Duncan. Why do you think Shakespeare changed this?

....

....

....

3 Women's role in society was quite limited in Shakespeare's day. There are just two women in the play, but they are presented very differently. What are the main differences between them? **Fill in the table** below:

	Lady Macbeth	Lady Macduff
a) *Her husband – what is he like?*		
b) *Her children (if any)*		
c) *Her actions*		
d) *How she dies*		

PROGRESS LOG [tick the correct box]   Needs more work ☐   Getting there ☐   Under control ☐

Settings

QUICK TEST

1 Look at the illustration below. Underneath each setting, **write the name(s)** of the **characters** and the **event(s)** in the play associated with it.

....

....

....

....

....

....

....

....

....

....

....

....

THINKING MORE DEEPLY

2 Write **three pieces of information** about the **settings** in these **scenes**:

Think about:

- Themes
- Plots
- Atmosphere

a) Act I Scene 1

Where it takes place: ....

Who it involves: ....

Why the setting is important: ....

b) Act III Scene 3

Where it takes place: ....

Who it involves: ....

Why the setting is important: ....

c) Act III Scene 4

Where it takes place: ....

Who it involves: ....

Why the setting is important: ....

3 Macbeth's castle is a **key location** in the play. **Complete** the following **grid** about the events that happen there:

Significant arrivals	
Murders	
Visions/ghosts	
Departures	

PROGRESS LOG [tick the correct box]   Needs more work ☐   Getting there ☐   Under control ☐

Practice task ⚡

1 First, **read** this **exam-style** task:

Read the section from *'KING: This castle hath a pleasant seat'* (Act I Scene 6 line 1) to *'The air is delicate.'* (line 10)

Question: Starting with this passage, explore the theme of betrayal. Refer closely to the passage in your answer and then write about the theme in the rest of the play.

2 Begin by circling the **key words** in the **question** above.

3 Now complete this table, noting down **3–4 key points** with **evidence** and the **effect** created:

Point	Evidence/quotation	Effect or explanation

4 Draft your response. Use the space below for your first paragraph(s) and then continue onto a sheet of paper:

Start: *In the opening to this scene, the King talks about his impressions of the Macbeth's castle. Firstly, he says that ...* ....

....

....

....

....

....

....

....

....

PROGRESS LOG [tick the correct box]   Needs more work ☐   Getting there ☐   Under control ☐

PART FIVE: FORM, STRUCTURE AND LANGUAGE

Form

QUICK TEST ✔

1 How many Acts is the play divided into?

    a) Five   b) Three   c) Four

2 Draw lines to link these stage directions to the relevant Act and scene:

'Thunder and lightning. Enter three Witches'   Act II Scene 3

'Enter a Porter. Knocking within'   Act III Scene 4

'Banquet prepared. Enter Macbeth, Lady Macbeth,
Ross, Lennox, Lords, and Attendants'   Act I Scene 1

3 Many scenes end with a pair of lines with rhymed words at the end. What are these called?

    a) Verse pairs   b) Rhyming couplets   c) Coupled prose

THINKING MORE DEEPLY ?

4 Complete this sentence:

Iambic .... is the dominant form in Shakespeare's verse. It

contains .... iambic feet, each one made up of two ....

The second is always ....

5 Think of an example from the first half of the play when Shakespeare uses prose, and explain why it is used:

....

....

....

....

6 In what ways are the witches' speeches different in form from the other types of verse and prose in the play?

....

....

....

....

....

PROGRESS LOG [tick the correct box]   Needs more work ☐   Getting there ☐   Under control ☐

Structure

QUICK TEST

1 Which of these are **TRUE** statements relating to the **structure** of events, and which are **FALSE**? Write 'T' or 'F' in the boxes:

a) Banquo does not appear after Act III Scene 3. ☐

b) Macbeth is at the height of his powers as the banquet scene starts. ☐

c) Lady Macbeth's power wanes in the second half of the play. ☐

d) The whole play takes place in Scotland. ☐

e) There are at least two violent deaths in every Act. ☐

2 Number these **soliloquies** so that they are in the **correct sequence** according to when they occur in the play. Use 1 for the first soliloquy, and 5 for the final one.

The Porter's speech before he opens the gate	
Lady Macbeth's 'milk of human kindness' speech while waiting for Macbeth	
Macbeth's speech weighing up the pros and cons of killing Duncan	
Macbeth's speech in which he reflects about Banquo being a threat to him	
Macbeth's 'dagger' speech as he is on his way to murder Duncan	

THINKING MORE DEEPLY

3 Look at this simple **line graph** based on Macbeth's reputation throughout the play, and a student's explanation alongside it:

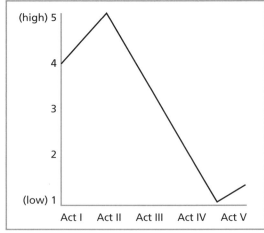

Macbeth's reputation (not power)

I think Macbeth's reputation is at its height in Act I Scene 6 as Duncan arrives at the Macbeths' castle. However, it falls to its lowest point when Macduff's family is murdered (Act IV Scene 3), before rising briefly when he fights to the death at the end.

Now make your own graph on a separate piece of paper showing Lady Macbeth's strength or Malcolm's power across the play. Then, complete the following paragraph:

Start: *I think Lady Macbeth/Malcom shows her/his strength most in ...*

EXAM PREPARATION: WRITING ABOUT STRUCTURE

First, reread the section from *'MALCOLM: I have spoke'* (Act I Scene 4 line 4) to *'MACBETH: Safe toward your love and honour.'* (line 28)

Question: How does Shakespeare foreshadow key events and ideas in this extract?

Think about:

● Malcolm and Duncan's comments on the Thane of Cawdor and Macbeth

● The later actions of Macbeth

4 Complete this table:

Point/detail	Evidence	Effect or explanation
1: *Malcolm explains the surprising manner of how the traitor Cawdor faced his execution.*	*'he … set forth / A deep repentance.' (lines 7–8)*	*This establishes the theme of a traitor's regret, and introduces the idea of people being difficult to 'read'.*
2: *Duncan says it is impossible to judge people from how they look.*		
3: *Macbeth pledges loyalty to Duncan, his family and followers.*		

5 Write up **point 1** into a **paragraph** below in your own words. Remember to include what you infer from the evidence, or the writer's effects:

....
....
....
....
....

6 Now choose **one** of your **other points** and write it out as another **paragraph** here:

....
....
....
....
....
....
....

PROGRESS LOG [tick the correct box]   Needs more work ☐   Getting there ☐   Under control ☐

Language

1 **Select** the **correct word** to complete these examples of **imagery** from the play:

a) Macbeth: 'The Thane of Cawdor lives. Why do you dress me / In borrowed ....?' (Act I Scene 3 lines 107–8)

  clothes   robes   cloaks

b) Macbeth: 'And Pity, like a .... new-born babe' (Act I Scene 7 line 21)

  naked   nasty   naive

c) Lady Macbeth: 'The sleeping and the dead / Are but as ....' (Act II Scene 2 lines 53–4)

  pictures   paintings   poetry

d) Macbeth: 'O, full of .... is my mind, dear wife!' (Act III Scene 2 line 36)

  serpents   spiders   scorpions

e) Ross: 'Alas, poor country … It cannot / Be called our mother, but our ....' (Act IV Scene 3 lines 164–6)

  godfather   grave   grace

2 Add further annotations to the following **quotation**, underlining the imagery used and making notes to explain its effect.

After the murder of their father, Malcolm and Donalbain decide to flee. Malcolm explains:

image of arrow shot by murderers of Duncan

'This murderous shaft that's shot

Hath not yet lighted; and our safest way

Is to avoid the aim.' **Act II Scene 3 lines 138–40**

('lighted' means 'landed')

THINKING MORE DEEPLY

❸ The following **motifs** run through the play, but they have many meanings. In each case give **two occasions** where the motif appears or is used, and **explain** what **different meanings or ideas** are connected to it:

a) SLEEP

Act .... Scene ....

Act .... Scene ....

Significance/effect/link to other ideas:

....

....

....

....

....

b) BLOOD

Act .... Scene ....

Act .... Scene ....

Significance/effect/link to other ideas:

....

....

....

....

....

c) WEATHER AND NATURE

Act .... Scene ....

Act .... Scene ....

Significance/effect/link to other ideas:

....

....

....

....

PROGRESS LOG [tick the correct box]   Needs more work ☐   Getting there ☐   Under control ☐

EXAM PREPARATION: WRITING ABOUT LANGUAGE

Language which **contrasts key ideas, events or people** is a key aspect in the play. How and why does Shakespeare use it?

Think about:

- The use of vocabulary and imagery
- How particular themes or ideas are juxtaposed

4 Complete this table:

Point/detail	Evidence	Effect or explanation
1: *Antithesis is used to convey the idea that characters can be deceptive.*	*'Fair is foul, and foul is fair.' (Act I Scene 1 line 9)*	*Characters who seem to be trustworthy – Cawdor, Macbeth and Lady Macbeth – turn out not to be so.*
2: *Nature imagery is used to show the world turned upside down.*		
3: *Evil and innocence are contrasted in speeches such as Lady Macbeth's when calling on the powers of darkness.*		

5 Write up **point 1** into a **paragraph** below in your own words. Remember to include what you infer from the evidence, or the writer's effects:

....

....

....

....

....

....

6 Now choose **one** of your **other points** and write it out as another **paragraph** here:

....

....

....

....

....

....

Practice task

1 First, **read** this **exam-style** task:

Read the extract beginning *'LADY MACBETH: How now, my lord?'* (Act III Scene 2 line 8) to *'MACBETH: There's comfort yet!'* (line 39)

Question: How does Shakespeare use language about disease or sickness in this extract, and at other times in the play?

Think about:

- Macbeth and Lady Macbeth's state of mind
- How Scotland is described

2 Begin by circling the **key words** in the **question** above.

3 Now complete the table, noting down **3–4 key points** with **evidence** and the **effect** created:

Point	Evidence/quotation	Effect or explanation

4 **Draft your response**. Use the space below for your first paragraph(s) and then continue onto a sheet of paper:

Start: *In this extract, Macbeth's mind is shown to be …*

PART SIX: Progress Booster

Writing skills

1) How well can you express your ideas about *Macbeth*? Look at this grid and tick the level you think you are currently at:

Level	How you respond	What your spelling, punctuation and grammar is like	Tick
Higher	• You analyse the effect of specific words and phrases very closely (i.e. 'zooming in' on them and exploring their meaning). • You select quotations very carefully and you embed them fluently in your sentences. • You are persuasive and convincing in the points you make, often coming up with original ideas.	You use a wide range of specialist terms (words like 'imagery'), excellent punctuation, accurate spelling, grammar, etc.	
Mid	• You analyse some parts of the text closely, but not all the time. • You support what you say with evidence and quotations, but sometimes your writing could be more fluent to read. • You make relevant comments on the text.	You use a good range of specialist terms, generally accurate punctuation, usually accurate spelling, grammar, etc.	
Lower	• You comment on some words and phrases but often you do not develop your ideas. • You sometimes use quotations to back up what you say but they are not always well chosen. • You mention the effect of certain words and phrases but these are not always relevant to the task.	You do not have a very wide range of specialist terms, but you have reasonably accurate spellings, punctuation and grammar.	

SELECTING AND USING QUOTATIONS

2) Read these two samples from students' responses to a question about how Banquo is presented. Decide which of the three levels they fit best, i.e. **lower** (L), **mid** (M) or **higher** (H).

Student A: *Banquo thinks a lot about what has happened. We are told he is worried about 'cursèd thoughts' (Act II Scene 1 line 8) which will come when he sleeps. This makes us think he is anxious about the witches' words.*

Level? ☐   Why? ....

....

Student B: *Shakespeare indicates Banquo's uneasiness when he reveals to his son that despite his tiredness he doesn't want to sleep because of the 'cursèd thoughts' that may come to him. Although this is stated before the murder, the adjective 'cursèd' suggests these thoughts are very troubling, and that he may already suspect Macbeth. This is also implied by him asking Fleance for his sword as they hear someone approach. It is Macbeth.*

Level? ☐   Why? ....

....

ZOOMING IN – YOUR TURN!

Here is the first part of another student response. The student has picked a good quotation but he hasn't 'zoomed in' on any particular words or phrases:

When Macbeth suggests that it would be in Banquo's interest to support him in the future, Banquo says he will keep his 'bosom franchised and allegiance clear' (Act II Scene 1 line 28) which reveals that he intends to remain independent.

3 Pick out one of the **words** or **phrases** the student has quoted and write a further sentence to complete the explanation:

The word/phrase '...................................' suggests that ....

....

....

EXPLAINING IDEAS

You need to be precise about the way Shakespeare gets ideas across. This can be done by varying your use of verbs (not just using 'says' or 'means').

4 Read this paragraph from a **mid-level** response to a question about Macbeth's relationship with Lady Macbeth. Circle all the **verbs** that are repeated in the student's writing (not in the quotation):

The scene shows that Macbeth is shocked by Lady Macbeth's ruthless ambition when he says, 'Bring forth men-children only!' (Act I Scene 7 line 72) This says that Lady Macbeth is more likely to produce men, traditionally more aggressive than girls. It also says that she is not a natural mother.

5 Now choose some of the words below to replace your circled ones:

suggests	implies	tells us	presents	signals	asks	demonstrates
	recognise	comprehend	reveals	conveys	indicates	

6 Rewrite your **Higher-level** version of the paragraph in full below. Remember to mention the **author by name** to show you understand he is **making choices** in how he presents characters, themes and events.

....
....
....
....
....
....
....
....

PROGRESS LOG [tick the correct box]　　Needs more work ☐　　Getting there ☐　　Under control ☐

Making inferences and interpretations

WRITING ABOUT INFERENCES

You need to be able to show you can read between the lines, and make inferences, rather than just explain more explicit 'surface' meanings.

Here is an extract from one student's **very good** response to a question about Macbeth's development and how this is presented:

In Act III Scene 4, Macbeth tells Lady Macbeth that he will do anything for 'mine own good', in other words do anything to keep himself safe. He also says that because he is in 'blood stepped in so far … returning were as tedious as go o'er' (lines 135–7): this is a metaphor which tells us that he might as well continue with violent acts as he has already committed so many. It also implies that he has become dehumanised; from now on he seems to act mechanically, as if racing towards his fate as there can be no turning back.

1 Look at the response carefully:

- **Underline** the simple point which explains what Macbeth feels.
- **Circle** the sentence that develops the first point.
- **Highlight** the sentence that shows an inference and begins to explore wider interpretations.

INTERPRETING – YOUR TURN!

2 Read the opening to this student response carefully and then **choose the point** from a), b) or c) which shows **inference** and could lead to **a deeper interpretation**. Remember – interpreting is *not* guesswork!

Macbeth reflects on his life and compares it to that of an actor who has only a short time to make his mark, 'a poor player / That struts and frets his hour upon the stage / And then is heard no more' (Act V Scene 5 lines 24–6). This indicates that life is short, and once we are gone we do not leave much of a mark. It also implies that …

    a) acting is a worthless profession which no one should choose

    b) he has not behaved well or played his role in life as he should have done

    c) he is angry and worried about life

3 Now, complete this **paragraph** about Macduff, adding your own final sentence which makes inferences or explores wider interpretations:

Malcolm is clearly aware of how treacherous Macbeth is. When he questions Macduff in Act IV Scene 3 he wonders if Macduff might be working for Macbeth, aiming to 'offer up a weak poor innocent lamb'. It also implies that Malcolm is unlike his father

because … ....

....

....

....

PROGRESS LOG [tick the correct box]   Needs more work ☐   Getting there ☐   Under control ☐

Writing about context

EXPLAINING CONTEXT

When you write about context you must make sure it is relevant to the task.

Read this comment by a student about Malcolm:

Malcolm's presentation of himself as someone who would 'delight / No less in truth than life' (Act IV Scene 3 lines 129–30) is designed to present a moral and pure king, in contrast with the usurper – Macbeth – who has stolen the crown and murdered for it. It could be seen as supporting the right of James I to be king, and a warning to those who might challenge him for the crown that they would be interfering with the divine order.

1 Why is this an **effective paragraph** about **context**?

a) It explains how decent Malcolm is.

b) It makes the link between the way Malcolm is presented and ideas of kingship in Shakespeare's time.

c) It tells us who was on the throne when *Macbeth* was performed.

YOUR TURN!

2 Now read this **further paragraph**, and complete it by **choosing a suitable point** from a), b) or c) related to context:

Macbeth's uncertainty about the promises made by the witches is evident in his words when he says, 'This supernatural soliciting / Cannot be ill, cannot be good'. He both mistrusts what he has been told, and yet also feels it has revealed truth in naming him Thane of Cawdor. This central theme of the power of supernatural forces reflects …

a) *how scary the play is to watch for us today with all the things they predict.*

b) *the way the whole play will be governed by whether the predictions turn out to be true and how they hide reality.*

c) *people's concerns at the time when rational or scientific explanations for natural disasters, illnesses and death were not available, and belief in demons and witches was quite widespread.*

3 Now, write a **paragraph** explaining how Shakespeare shows that tyrants such as Macbeth eventually fail and have to answer for their crimes:

Shakespeare shows that tyrants and dictators cannot be allowed to win by showing

how, towards the end of the play, … ....

....

....

....

....

PROGRESS LOG [tick the correct box]   Needs more work ☐   Getting there ☐   Under control ☐

Structure and linking of paragraphs (A01) (A04)

Paragraphs need to demonstrate your points clearly by:

● Using **topic sentences**

● Focusing on **key words** from quotations

● Explaining their **effect** or meaning

1 Read this model paragraph in which a student explains how Shakespeare presents Duncan:

Shakespeare presents Duncan as a saintly, well-respected king. Even Macbeth when thinking about murdering him is forced to accept that 'his virtues / Will plead like angels' (Act I Scene 7 lines 18–19). The use of the nouns 'virtues' and 'angels' links Duncan to divine or heavenly character traits, and therefore makes Macbeth's potential murder of him all the more sinful.

Look at the paragraph carefully:

● **Underline** the topic sentence which explains the main point about Duncan.

● **Circle** the words that are picked out from the quotation.

● **Highlight** the part of the last sentence which explains the words.

2 Now read this **paragraph** by a student who is explaining how Shakespeare presents Lady Macbeth in the later part of the play:

We find out about Lady Macbeth when she is sleepwalking as she says 'What, will these hands ne'er be clean?' (Act V Scene 1 line 42). This tell us that she feels guilty about the murderous acts she has been involved in.

Expert viewpoint: This paragraph could be more precise. It does not begin with a topic sentence to explain how Shakespeare presents Lady Macbeth and doesn't zoom in on any key words that tell us what she is like, or explain the effect of the chosen words.

Now **rewrite the paragraph**. Start with a **topic sentence**, and pick out a **key word or phrase** to 'zoom in' on, then follow up with an explanation or interpretation:

Shakespeare presents Lady Macbeth in this scene as … ....

....

....

....

....

....

....

....

....

....

....

It is equally important to make your sentences link together and your ideas follow on fluently from each other. You can do this by:

● Using a mixture of short and long sentences as appropriate
● Using words or phrases that help connect or develop ideas

3 Read this model paragraph by one student writing about how Lady Macduff is presented:

Shakespeare presents Lady Macduff as an isolated, innocent mother who acts as a contrast to Lady Macbeth. She is initially shown as independent of thought, questioning her husband's motives, saying his 'flight was madness' (Act IV Scene 2 line 3) and even telling her son, only partly in jest, that his father was a 'traitor' (line 45). However, later in the scene it is her vulnerability that is most powerful. When the messenger appears, her simple question, 'Whither should I fly?' (line 73) implies she has nowhere to go, and nowhere to turn.

Look at the response carefully:

● **Underline** the topic sentence which introduces the main idea.
● **Underline** the short sentence which signals a change in ideas.
● **Circle** any words or phrases that link ideas such as 'who', 'when', 'firstly', 'which', etc.

4 Read this **paragraph** by another student also commenting on how Lady Macduff is presented:

Shakespeare presents us with a sympathetic portrayal of Lady Macduff. The messenger appears and warns her about danger. He says, 'Hence with your little ones!' (Act IV Scene 2 line 69). This tells us that the children are in Macbeth's sights. It reminds us of the fragile nature of life. Her simple statement, 'I have done no harm' (line 74) emphasises her innocence. The murderers come in and accuse her husband of treason.

Expert viewpoint: The candidate has understood how the character's nature is revealed. However, the paragraph is rather awkwardly written. It needs improving by linking the sentences with suitable phrases and joining words such as 'when', 'where', 'and', 'later', 'finally', etc.

Rewrite the **paragraph**, improving the **style**, and also try to add a **concluding sentence** summing up how she is portrayed in this part of the scene.

Start with the same **topic sentence**:

Shakespeare presents us with a sympathetic portrayal of Lady Macduff. When ...

PROGRESS LOG [tick the correct box]   Needs more work ☐   Getting there ☐   Under control ☐

Spelling, punctuation and grammar

Here are a number of key words you might use when writing in the exam:

Content and structure	Characters and style	Linguistic features
Act	character	metaphor
scene	role	personification
quotation	protagonist	juxtaposition
sequence	dramatic	dramatic irony
dialogue	tragedy	repetition
climax	villainous	symbol
development	humorous	monologue
stage directions	sympathetic	euphemism
verse	minor (character)	soliloquy

1 Circle any you might find difficult to spell, and then use the 'Look, Say, Cover, Write, Check' method to learn them. This means: **look** at the word; **say** it out loud; then **cover** it up; **write** it out (without looking at it!); uncover and **check** your spelling with the correct version.

2 Create a **mnemonic** for five of your difficult spellings. For example:

tragedy: **t**en **r**eally **a**ngry **g**irls **e**njoyed **d**ancing **y**esterday!

Or

break the word down: T – RAGE – DY!

a) ....

b) ....

c) ....

d) ....

e) ....

3 Circle any **incorrect spellings** in this paragraph and then rewrite it:

At the end of Act I, the tention builds dramataically as Macbeth clames he has 'no spur' for killing Dunkin. In his dialog with Lady Macbeth it is clear he is uncertain weather to proceed with the murder and it is only when his wife condemns him for not being a man, that he rises to the challenge. By the time the curtain falls, Shakspeare ensures that the audiense knows that Macbeth is 'settled' on commiting this 'terrible feet'.

....

....

....

....

Punctuation can help make your meaning clear.

Here is one response by a student commenting on Shakespeare's use of the term 'sisters' for the witches. Check for correct use of:

- Apostrophes
- Speech marks for quotations and emphasis
- Full stops, commas and capital letters

When shakespeare refers to the witches as the weird sisters he is suggesting that they form a close blood bond as if they were one entity rather than three separate people this gives their speech extra power almost as if each time they speak it could be one voice for example, in act 1 scene 1 we see shakespeare's decision to separate their three lines 'I come, grey-malkin', 'Paddock calls', and 'Anon!' (line 9) but rhythmically allow it to be structured as if a single line of speech.

④ Rewrite it **correctly** here:

....
....
....
....
....
....

⑤ It is better to use the **present tense** to describe what is happening in the play.

Look at these two extracts. Which one uses tenses **consistently** and **accurately**?

Student A: *Shakespeare suggested to us through the variety of places and situations in which Ross appeared that he is quite a political, almost slippery character who changes as the wind changed. He was not to be trusted.*

Student B: *Shakespeare suggests to us through the variety of places and situations in which Ross appears that he is quite a political, almost slippery character who changes as the wind changes. He is not to be trusted.*

⑥ Now look at this further paragraph. Underline or circle all its verb **tenses** first:

Shakespeare decided to make Ross the character who is present with Lady Macduff as Act IV Scene 2 opened. He kept his views to himself and refuses to answer her questions directly, and said, 'I dare not speak much further' (line 17), which implies he knew what was about to happen.

Now rewrite it using the **present tense** consistently:

....
....
....
....
....
....
....
....

PROGRESS LOG [tick the correct box]   Needs more work ☐   Getting there ☐   Under control ☐

Tackling exam tasks

It is important to be able to identify key words in exam tasks and then quickly generate some ideas.

Read this task and notice how the key words have been underlined:

Read from *'KING: My worthy Cawdor!'* (Act I Scene 4 line 48) to *'It is a peerless kinsman.'* (line 59)

Question: <u>In what ways</u> does <u>Shakespeare</u> <u>present</u> <u>Macbeth</u> as <u>ambitious</u>:

● In <u>this extract</u>

● In the <u>play as a whole</u>?

1 Now do the same with this task, i.e. **underline** the **key words**:

Read from *'LADY MACBETH: Yet here's a spot'* (Act V Scene 1 lines 31) to *'To bed, to bed, to bed.'* (line 64)

Question: Explain how Shakespeare explores Lady Macbeth's conscience:

● In this extract

● In the play as a whole

2 Now you need to generate ideas quickly. Use the spider-diagram* below and add as many ideas of your own as you can:

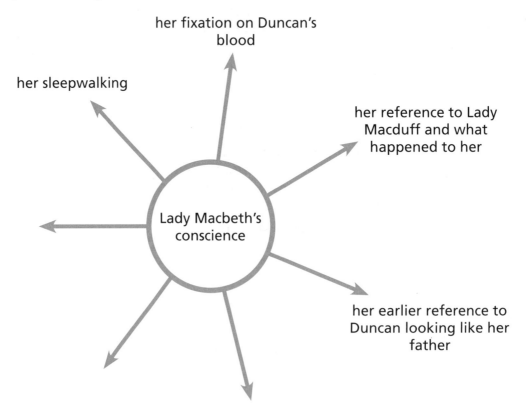

her fixation on Duncan's blood

her sleepwalking

her reference to Lady Macduff and what happened to her

Lady Macbeth's conscience

her earlier reference to Duncan looking like her father

*You can do this as a list if you wish.

PLANNING AN ESSAY

3 Here is the exam-style task from the previous page:

Read from *'LADY MACBETH: Yet here's a spot'* (Act V Scene 1 lines 31) to *'To bed, to bed, to bed.'* (line 64)

Question: Explain how Shakespeare explores Lady Macbeth's conscience:

- In this extract
- In the play as a whole

Using the ideas you generated, write a simple **plan** with at least **five key points** (the first two have been done for you). Check back to your spider diagram or the list you made:

a) *Shakespeare explores the idea that Lady Macbeth cannot rid herself of the image of Duncan's blood.*

b) *He demonstrates how she cannot stop thinking of Lady Macduff's murder.*

c) ....

d) ....

e) ....

4 Now list **five quotations**, one for each point (the first two have been provided for you):

a) *'LADY MACBETH: Yet who would have thought the old man to have had so much blood in him'* (lines 38–9)

b) *'LADY MACBETH: The Thane of Fife had a wife; where is she now?'* (line 41)

c) ....

d) ....

e) ....

5 Now read this task and write a **plan** of your own, including **quotations**, on a separate sheet of paper. (The key words have been underlined.)

Read from *'KING: My worthy Cawdor!'* (Act I Scene 4 line 48) to *'It is a peerless kinsman.'* (line 59)

Question: In what ways does Shakespeare present Macbeth as ambitious:

- In this extract
- In the play as a whole?

PROGRESS LOG [tick the correct box]   Needs more work ☐   Getting there ☐   Under control ☐

Sample answers

OPENING PARAGRAPHS

Here is one of the tasks from earlier:

Read from *'LADY MACBETH: Yet here's a spot'* (Act V Scene 1 lines 31) to *'To bed, to bed, to bed.'* (line 64)

Question: Explain how Shakespeare explores Lady Macbeth's conscience:

- In this extract
- In the play as a whole

Now look at these two alternate openings to the essay and read the expert viewpoints underneath:

Student A

> *Shakespeare presents Lady Macbeth's conscience as something that develops as the play progresses. As the play opens, she seems to be fixated on gaining power for herself and Macbeth. However, as the play progresses we get hints about another side of her.*

Student B

> *Lady Macbeth starts the play as a really evil person. She plans the murders and is as ruthless as Macbeth. She doesn't feel much guilt to start with. She is the one who sorts out the daggers when Macbeth is too frightened to take them back into the bedchamber.*

Expert viewpoint 1: This is a clear opening paragraph that outlines Lady Macbeth's 'journey' as a human being over the course of the play. It suggests she undergoes a change according to the effect of murderous acts. However, it could say a little more about that other 'side' to her which we learn about.

Expert viewpoint 2: This opening recounts what happens at the start of the play and what Lady Macbeth does but it doesn't outline what the essay will cover, or the key area of her presentation across the whole play.

1 Which comment belongs to which answer? Match the paragraph (A or B) to the expert's feedback (1 or 2).

Student A: .... **Student B:** ....

2 Now it's your turn. Write the opening paragraph to this task on a separate sheet of paper:

Read from *'KING: My worthy Cawdor!'* to *'It is a peerless kinsman.'* (Act I Scene 4 lines 48–59)

Question: In what ways does Shakespeare present Macbeth as ambitious:

- In this extract
- In the play as a whole?

Remember:

- Introduce the topic in general terms, perhaps **explaining** or **'unpicking'** the key **words** or **ideas** in the task (such as 'present').
- Mention the **different possibilities** or ideas that you are going to address.
- Use the **author's name**.

WRITING ABOUT TECHNIQUES

Here are two paragraphs in response to a different task, where the students have focused on the writer's techniques. The task is:

Read from *'BANQUO: Thou hast it now'* (Act III Scene 1 line 1) to *'My lord, I will not'* (line 28).

Question: How does Shakespeare present Banquo as ambitious:

- In this scene
- In the play as a whole?

Student A

> Banquo says that he is worried that Macbeth: *'thou playedst most foully'* to become king, which shows that he understands enough about power to see that sometimes people will murder to get what they want. Shakespeare's use of the phrase *'I fear'* suggests that Banquo himself would not go as far.

Student B

> Shakespeare fills Banquo's speech with ambiguous statements that leave the audience uncertain about how genuine he is. Banquo's comment about Macbeth in which he says, *'I fear thou playedst most foully'* in order to become king could suggest that he himself would never go as far as murder, which could show him as less ambitious than Macbeth. Yet the verb could also imply personal *'fear'* – that his life is in danger because Macbeth thinks he is ambitious. After all, unlike Macbeth, Banquo was not rewarded by Duncan for his bravery in battle.

Expert viewpoint 1: This higher-level response comments on a specific quotation but it explores more than one inference from the specific word selected. The second sentence is a little long, but develops the possible interpretation before the final sentences go further and then link to other moments from the play.

Expert viewpoint 2: This mid-level response highlights the effect of one statement on our understanding of Banquo. However, the quotation, though appropriate, is not sufficiently embedded in the sentence, and there is not much in the way of development or exploration of what is said in order to consider other possibilities.

❸ Which comment belongs to which answer? Match the paragraph (A or B) to the examiner feedback (1 or 2).

Student A: .... **Student B:** ....

❹ Now, take another **aspect** of this or a different scene and on a separate sheet of paper write your own **paragraph**. You could **comment** on one of these aspects:

- Banquo's recollection of the witches prophecy about his children
- Banquo's dreaming about the witches (Act II Scene 1)
- Banquo's refusal to directly confirm he would support Macbeth (Act II Scene 1)

5 Now read this **lower-level** response to the following task:

Read from *'LADY MACBETH: Who was it that thus cried?'* (Act II Scene 2 line 44) to *'Be not lost so poorly in your thoughts.'* (lines 71–2)

Question: How does Shakespeare present Lady Macbeth as a powerful woman in this extract?

Student response:

> *When Macbeth is upset and can't face what he has done, Lady Macbeth shows she is powerful because she criticises him for showing weakness, 'Why, worthy thane, you do unbend your noble strength, to think so brainsickly of things.' This means she thinks he is not strong like he was before. He should not allow things to get to him. This is weird when you think about how she acts later in the play.*
>
> *She shows her power by giving lots of orders. She realises he has not carried out the plan properly and she tells him what he has to do. This is to take the daggers back.*

Expert viewpoint: The quotation in the first paragraph is well chosen and gives us a sense of how she criticises Macbeth but it is not embedded in the sentence. Nor is there any real focus on the effect of particular words or phrases. The language the student uses is sometimes too informal, as in 'weird' and 'gets to him'.

Rewrite these two **paragraphs**, improving them by addressing:

- The lack of development of linking of points – no **'zooming in'** on **key words and phrases**
- The lack of **embedding in the first paragraph and quotation in the second**
- No **specialist terms** (could you use 'ironic'?) and use of **informal vocabulary**

Paragraph 1:

In this scene, Shakespeare presents Lady Macbeth as ....

....

and also ....

....

This implies that ....

....

However, this is .... *because later in the play* ....

....

Paragraph 2:

Lady Macbeth's use of language shows the power that she has, for example ....

....

Overall, this shows her ....

....

A FULL-LENGTH RESPONSE

6 Write a full-length response to this exam-style task on a separate sheet of paper. Answer both parts of the question:

Read from *'MACBETH: Seyton! – I am sick at heart'* (Act V Scene 3 line 19) to *'I'll put it on.'* (line 34)

Question: How is Macbeth presented as a tragic figure:

● In this extract

● In the play as a whole?

Remember to do the following:

● Plan **quickly** (no more than 5 minutes) jotting down **4 or 5 supporting quotations**.

● Refer closely to the **key words** in the question.

● Make sure you comment on **what** the writer does, the **techniques** he uses and the **effect** of those techniques.

● Support your points with **well-chosen quotations** or other evidence.

● Develop your points by **'zooming in'** on particular **words** or **phrases** and explaining their **effect**.

● Be **persuasive** and **convincing** in what you say.

● Check carefully for **spelling**, **punctuation** and **grammar**.

PROGRESS LOG [tick the correct box]   Needs more work ☐   Getting there ☐   Under control ☐

Further questions   (A01)(A02)(A03)(A04)

1 How is Macduff presented as a figure of revenge in the final scene of the play, and in the play as a whole?

2 Read from *'MALCOLM: The king-becoming graces'* (Act IV Scene 3 line 91) to *'MACDUFF: Thy hope ends here!'* (line 114).

Question: How is the idea of an ideal king explored here, and in the rest of the play?

3 What is the dramatic significance of Act IV Scene 1? Think about:

● What Macbeth learns

● How he responds to what he sees and hears

4 Read from *'MACBETH: What man dare, I dare.'* (Act III Scene 4 line 98) to *'mine is blanched with fear.'* (line 115)

Question: How does Shakespeare explore the idea of Macbeth's manliness here and elsewhere in the play?

5 To what extent do you think the supernatural is to blame for Macbeth's downfall?

PROGRESS LOG [tick the correct box]   Needs more work ☐   Getting there ☐   Under control ☐

ANSWERS

NOTE: Answers have been provided for most tasks. Exceptions are 'Practice tasks' and tasks which ask you to write a paragraph or to use your own words or judgement.

PART TWO: PLOT AND ACTION [pp. 8–38]

Act I Scenes 1 and 2 [pp. 8–9]

1 a) T; b) F; c) T; d) T; e) F; f) F; g) F

2 a) Witches' spells and chanting would be dramatic, as would stormy weather. The audience will want to know more about battle and Macbeth.

b) Macdonwald is 'worthy' but has 'villainies of nature'. Thane of Cawdor is a traitor who turned against Duncan

c) He is a Captain, equal to Macbeth. He fought bravely alongside him

3

Point/detail	Evidence	Effect or explanation
1: We learn that Macbeth is a powerful and skilful warrior.	'his brandished steel, / Which smoked with bloody execution' (lines 17–18)	His sword seemed to be on fire he used it so expertly.
2: He is shown to be courageous despite the danger.	Macbeth is compared to an 'eagle' and 'lion'; is also called 'Brave Macbeth'.	Despite the odds against him and Banquo, they triumphed.
3: He is merciless.	Macbeth 'unseamed him from the nave to the chops, / And fixed his head upon our battlements'.	Macbeth cut Macdonwald from the stomach to the jaw and then chopped his head off!

Act I Scenes 3 and 4 [pp. 10–11]

1 a) They have beards; b) 'Thane of Cawdor' and 'King hereafter'; c) Banquo; d) Malcolm; e) Inverness

2 a) As far as he is aware the Thane of Cawdor is alive and well. He doesn't know he is a traitor.

b) Banquo tells Macbeth that the 'instruments of darkness' sometimes tell people things they want to hear. However, they use them to make them commit evil acts.

c) He comments on Malcolm ('Prince of Cumberland') being named heir and his need to overcome this obstacle. He also talks about his 'black and deep desires' which suggest evil, hidden forces.

3

Point/detail	Evidence	Effect or explanation
1: Witches tell Macbeth he is Thane of Cawdor and will soon be king.	'be king hereafter' (line 49)	The promise of present and future power sows a seed in Macbeth's mind.
2: Language is used to develop the idea that things may not be what they seem.	Banquo: 'why do you … seem to fear / Things that do sound so fair?'	These opposites, also in the references to the two men, 'lesser … greater' show that finding the truth is difficult.
3: Macbeth and Banquo are shown to promise different things, suggesting they are potential rivals.	The witches say Banquo 'shalt get kings, though thou be none.'	Macbeth has already been told he will be king, so saying Banquo will give birth to kings suggests a problem that will need to be resolved.

Act I Scenes 4 and 5 [pp. 12–13]

1 a) Lady Macbeth receives a letter from him; b) She is told the King is coming to stay; c) 'Unsex' her (make her masculine); d) 'look like th'innocent flower'.

2 a) She calls him 'great' and 'worthy' and he refers to her as his 'dearest love'.

b) Lady Macbeth calls on 'spirits' to make her less feminine. She seems to plead with the powers of darkness and night (traditionally associated with the spirit world) to strengthen her.

c) She has already stated that she's going to 'pour her spirits' (persuade) Macbeth about what needs to be done when he returns. When he does return she tells Macbeth how to behave and that she will organise everything for the evening to come ('into my despatch').

3

Point/detail	Evidence	Effect or explanation
1: Lady Macbeth is concerned about the more gentle side of Macbeth's nature.	'too full o'the'milk of human-kindness'	This suggests Macbeth has a womanly, nurturing side – like the one Lady Macbeth tries to get rid of in herself.
2: She recognises his ambition, but fears he is too passive and won't act.	'What thou wouldst highly / That wouldst thou holily, wouldst not play false, / And yet wouldst wrongly win.'	She doesn't believe that power can come to them by behaving decently ('highly') so could be seen to be more realistic than him.
3: She worries that he shows his feelings too openly and needs to hide them.	'Your face … is as a book where men / May read strange matters.'	She feels he is an 'open book' and will reveal his ambition through how he looks.

Act I Scenes 6 and 7 [pp. 14–15]

1 a) 4; b) 6; c) 7; d) 5; e) 2; f) 1; g) 3

2 a) Banquo mistakenly believes Macbeth's castle is pleasant and welcoming because a bird associated with 'temples' (churches, etc.) has been seen there. He also mentions the air is like 'heaven's breath' yet this is where Duncan will be murdered and go to 'heaven'.

b) She says that if she had made a promise to do something so important she would have suppressed her motherly instincts and 'dashed' the brains of her baby on the ground.

c) The reference to the Macbeths disguising their real feelings – putting on 'fairest show' – echoes the 'foul is fair' couplet spoken by the witches.

3

Point/detail	Evidence	Effect or explanation
1: *Duncan is a decent, honest man.*	*'borne his faculties so meek, hath been / So clear in his great office' (lines 17–18)*	*Duncan represents a gentle, moral king, but is he weak?*
2: *Killing Duncan will highlight and exaggerate his strong points.*	*'his virtues / Will plead like angels, trumpet-tongued'*	*Macbeth is bound to suffer by comparison, however effective he might be.*
3: *Kings were often associated with religious imagery.*	*'Pity ... like heaven's cherubin ... Shall blow the horrid deed in every eye.'*	*By using the image of a child-trumpeter (like the ones in religious paintings) Macbeth reminds the audience of the divine right of kings.*

Act II Scenes 1 and 2 [pp. 16–17]

1 Scene 1 begins with Banquo giving Macbeth a **diamond** to pass to Lady Macbeth from Duncan. Macbeth is left alone and then sees an imaginary **dagger** which seems to be showing him the way to Duncan's **bedchamber/quarters**. Despite his doubts, he presses ahead as he hears the sound of a **bell**. Once he has committed the murder, we find out he has foolishly brought the **blood**-smeared weapons he used back with him. Lady Macbeth is furious with him, and she takes them back so she can smear the **grooms/ servants** so they look as they killed the king. She returns with blood on her own **hands.**

2 a) He refuses to commit himself, saying he wishes to keep his 'allegiance clear'.

  b) He tries to grab hold of it, and even sees blood on the blade. When it moves in the air it almost seems alive, leading him towards Duncan's rooms.

  c) She is jumpy and nervous, but has managed to give herself strength by drinking some of the alcohol the servants were given.

3

Point/detail	Evidence	Effect or explanation
1: *Shakespeare's use of questions shows uncertainty.*	*'Who's there?' (line 8)* *'Did not you speak?' (line 16)*	*The questions suggest their fear of being discovered, of being heard.*
2: *Short, sometimes one-word, lines one after another show the Macbeths depending on each other.*	*'Did not you speak?'* *'When?'* *'Now.'* *'Ay', etc.*	*A breathless, tense tone is created as they answer each other's questions.*
3: *Macbeth is obsessed with the sleeping grooms, and what they say.*	*He wonders why he couldn't say 'Amen' like the grooms.*	*Macbeth suggests prayer is not possible when you have committed murder.*

Act II Scenes 3 and 4 [pp. 18–19]

1 a) Macduff and Lennox; b) 'Unruly'; c) Macduff; d) They decide to leave immediately; e) Scone

2 a) It adds some rude humour and jokes, and so lightens the tension before the discovery of the murder.

  b) Chimneys were blown down in the wind. There were terrible wails and cries and even the earth seemed to be 'feverous' and shook.

  c) He refers to Duncan's body as the 'Lord's anointed temple' and calls the murder 'sacriligeous', meaning going against everything that is sacred and to be respected.

3

Point/detail	Evidence	Effect or explanation
1: *The scene recaps what happened to the grooms; tells us that the king's sons have fled; and sows the seeds of future conflict.*	*The ones who did the deed, were 'Those that Macbeth hath slain' (line 23)* *The sons are 'stolen away' (line 26)*	*It tells us that, for now, Macbeth has 'got away with it', but the rightful heir is still alive.*
2: *Macduff is not going to Macbeth's corronation.*	*'Will you to Scone?'* *'No, cousin, I'll to Fife.'*	*Macduff is hinting that he does not want to be seen to support Macbeth; this hints at the conflict to come.*
3: *The way nature has behaved reflects how the divine order has been disrupted.*	*'A falcon, towering in her pride of place / Was by a mousing owl hawked at and killed.'*	*This symbolises what has happened – a bird who should be less powerful (an owl) has killed a falcon; in the same way, a less important lord, Macbeth, has killed Duncan.*

Act III Scene 1 [pp. 20–1]

1 a) 2; b) 1; c) 4; d) 6; e) 3; f) 5; g) 7

2 a) He suspects that Macbeth was involved in the murder of Duncan yet he doesn't seem to have acted on this knowledge – perhaps he is waiting for an offer from Macbeth who has asked for his support in Act II Scene 1. He reflects about his own future and that he would be the father to 'many kings'.

  b) He realises that Banquo is intelligent (has 'wisdom') and will try to look after his own interests. He remembers how Banquo wanted to know his own future from the witches and that they said he'd be king, and hates the idea of Banquo's children benefiting from his murder of Duncan.

  c) Macbeth and Banquo have mutual 'friends' and Macbeth needs their support; if these friends thought Macbeth had exiled Banquo they might take Banquo's side, so Macbeth concludes it is better to have him murdered by hired killers.

3

Point/detail	Evidence	Effect or explanation
1: *Macbeth refers to past treatment of the men by Banquo.*	'held you / So under fortune, which you thought had been / Our innocent self.' (lines 76–8)	The men were deceived into thinking it was Macbeth who hadn't promoted or helped them in life.
2: *He questions their manhood using persuasive devices.*	He says they can avoid being in 'the worst rank of manhood' if they kill Banquo and can raise themselves up from being common 'dogs'.	He uses some of the same methods his wife used on him, mocking their manhood.
3: *There is no mention of Lady Macbeth's involvement.*	'I will advise you'	Macbeth makes it clear he will tell the murderers what they need to do.

Act III Scenes 2 and 3 [pp. 22–3]

1 a) T; b) F; c) F; d) T; e) T; e) T; f) F

2 a) His appeal to the 'night' is rather like Lady Macbeth's in Act I Scene 5 when she called on the powers of darkness to 'unsex' her. He uses the imperative verb 'Come' which sounds like him calling dark powers to appear.

b) He refers to 'night's black agents' which could also refer to the murderers. He speaks in a poetic way, referring to travellers reaching their place of rest – it is almost philosophical and does not seem to have much to do with the murder.

c) Banquo's death fulfils the prophecy that he is 'lesser' than Macbeth as he can now never be king. Fleance's escape means that Banquo's children could still become kings one day, however unlikely it may seem now.

3

Point/detail	Evidence	Effect or explanation
1: *Macbeth seems to be the one giving instructions.*	'Let your remembrance apply to Banquo' (line 30)	Macbeth advises Lady Macbeth on how to pretend all is well with Banquo. Earlier it was the other way around.
2: *Macbeth's last speech is similar to Lady Macbeth's in Act I Scene 5, showing his cold-blooded nature.*	'Come, seeling night'; 'night's black agents'	His appeal to the powers of darkness seems to be similar to her appeal to strengthen her resolve in Act I.
3: *He doesn't share his plans for Banquo with his wife.*	'Be innocent of the knowledge, dearest chuck, till thou applaud the deed.'	It is almost as if he is saying how pleasantly surprised she will be when she finds out about the murder.

Act III Scene 4 [pp. 24–5]

1 a) First murderer; b) Macbeth; c) She says it's a childhood illness; d) Macduff; e) He has a paid spy in each of their houses

2 a) They are able to celebrate being king and queen at a banquet for all the important lords. Duncan's sons are out of the way, and Macbeth believes that his main rival Banquo and his son are dead (though he soon learns that this is not the case).

b) She says a woman's winter story passed down from her grandmother told round a fire would be more frightening. Also, that he is 'unmanned' – no longer a man.

c) He says he has caused so much blood through his murders that going back now and facing what he's done would be as bad as carrying on.

3

Point/detail	Evidence	Effect or explanation
1: *This is the first of the visions related to Banquo and kingship.*	'Here is a place reserved, sir.' (line 45)	Banquo's ghost sits in Macbeth's place, reminding us that his children will ultimately inherit the throne, something we see enacted again in Act IV Scene 1.
2: *Visions related to the murder are seen only by Macbeth.*	'This is the very painting of your fear.'	Lady Macbeth believes the visions arise from Macbeth's fear or guilt over what he has done – later she will have her own visions.
3: *The supernatural has the capacity to violently disturb as well as to encourage.*	'Take any shape but that, and my firm nerves / Shall never tremble'	Macbeth wanted Banquo dead but now cannot face the reality of the prophecy, the gory phantom sitting at the table.

Act III Scenes 5 and 6 [pp. 26–7]

1 a) F; b) T; c) F; d) T; e) T; f) F

2 a) The rhythm of the lines suggests it might not have been written by Shakespeare. It does not add anything specific to the action, but is included more for theatrical colour and variety.

b) The fact that neutral lords (not Macduff) are referring to him as 'tyrant' – a type of violent dictator – suggests this is the common view, which has now developed from the respect and honour he had at the start, and even in the banquet scene.

c) We find out that Malcolm is in England, and that it is generally accepted Macbeth has stopped him from being rightful king. We find out Macduff is trying to get Northumberland and Seyward to join an army to depose Macbeth. Macbeth is preparing for war as a result.

3

Point/detail	Evidence	Effect or explanation
1: *Lennox uses guarded language to express doubts about Banquo's murder.*	'Whom you may say, if't please you, Fleance killed, / For Fleance fled.' (lines 6–7)	The phrase 'if't please you' suggests that this is not based on reality but what Macbeth would like you to think.
2: *He uses irony to criticise Macbeth about killing the servants.*	'Did he not straight – in pious rage – the two delinquents tear?' 'Was that not nobly done?'	By posing these questions, Lennox leaves the possibility of disagreeing 'hanging in the air'. Using the word 'pious' (religiously decent) is the opposite of what Macbeth is in reality.
3: *He hints that he is pleased Duncan's sons have not been captured by Macbeth.*	'they should find / What 'twere to kill a father'	Macbeth would have them executed as murderers of their own father – very conveniently.

Act IV Scenes 1 and 2 [pp. 28–9]

1 a) With the witches' spells; b) 'None of woman born'; c) Eight;
d) Ross; e) A traitor

2 a) Macbeth talks of things such as destroying corn, trees, castles, palaces and pyramids.

b) When he hears that 'none of woman born' can harm him, he says he will 'make assurance double sure', in other words kill Macduff so that he doesn't have to rely on the prophecy.

c) He tries to avoid seeing them – 'I'll see no more' – and calls them a 'Horrible sight!' He calls the time he has spent 'accursed' and 'pernicious', both negative adjectives.

3

Point/detail	Evidence	Effect or explanation
1: Lady Macduff suggests that her husband has abandoned them – which has some truth in it.	'for the poor wren ... will fight ... against the owl.' (lines 9–11)	This analogy, which links Lady Macduff and her children to tiny birds who stand up to a cruel predator, makes us sympathise with her plight.
2: Ross describes the current state of the world and how difficult it is to survive.	'float upon a wild and violent sea'	The metaphor suggests that life's journey is unpredictable and rough.
3: Lady Macduff's son says he isn't afraid.	'Poor birds they are not set for'	The boy's innocence is shown in his continuation of the analogy. He suggests small, weak birds are of no interest to predators; we know Macbeth has given orders which show the opposite.

Act IV Scene 3 [pp. 30–1]

1 a) 5; b) 3; c) 1; d) 4; e) 2; f) 7; g) 6

2 a) Malcolm wonders why Macduff hasn't been harmed or attacked by Macbeth. He is surprised that Macduff has left the land and family he cares so much about given that Scotland is suffering under Macbeth's rule.

b) He says that 'each minute' a new 'grief' is discovered – a hint at the news he is about to tell. He tells Macduff they were 'well at peace' when he left them (which could mean 'unharmed' but also dead, as in resting in peace).

c) Ross calls them 'murdered deer'. Macduff refers to them as 'pretty chickens and their dam'.

3

Point/detail	Evidence	Effect or explanation
1: Malcolm's description of himself creates a contrast with Macbeth's cruelty.	'My first false speaking / Was this upon myself.' (lines 130–1)	Malcolm's pretending to be evil is the first time he's been dishonest – Macbeth's 'false-speaking' has been shown many times.
2: Edward's healing ability underlines the divine right of kings.	'To the succeeding royalty he leaves / The healing benediction'	Malcolm says that his heirs will inherit his miraculous powers, which highlights the importance of rightful succession.
3: Edward's saintliness reminds us of Duncan.	He 'solicits heaven' and is 'full of grace'	Macbeth's speech in Act I Scene 7 contains references to 'angels' and 'heaven' when speaking about Duncan, stressing the idea of divine right.

Act V Scene 1 [pp. 32–3]

1 a) F; b) T; c) T; d) F; e) T; f) T; g) F

2 a) It is an informal, private conversation between the Doctor and Gentlewoman. The prose allows Lady Macbeth's speech to be broken up into fragments and short, blurted out statements which is how someone might talk in their sleep.

b) She was furious with Macbeth for not having the strength to go back into Duncan's quarters to put blood on the daggers. She told him how easy it was to get rid of the blood on their hands: 'A little water clears us of this deed' (Act II Scene 3).

c) Lady Macbeth needs help which is beyond him, 'beyond my practice', i.e. religious or spiritual, rather than medical, help: 'More needs she the divine than the physician.'

3

Point/detail	Evidence	Effect or explanation
1: Lady Macbeth's earlier comments about Duncan looking like her father affected her more than we thought.	'Yet who would have thought the old man to have had so much blood in him?' (lines 38–9)	Lady Macbeth is fixated on and horrified by the amount of blood that has been spilt.
2: Shakespeare suggests that guilt cannot be easily removed.	'All the perfumes of Arabia will not sweeten this little hand.'	This is in effect a metaphor: 'sweeten' here means 'remove the stain of murder'.
3: Her words ironically echo her earlier arguments to persuade Macbeth in Act II Scene 2.	'A soldier and afeard? What need we fear...?' and 'I tell you yet again, Banquo's buried; he cannot come out on's grave.'	The 'fear' in the end comes not from enemies but from inside her.

ANSWERS

Act V Scenes 2 and 3 [pp. 34–5]

1 a) Donalbain; b) 'dwarfish thief'; c) 10,000; d) 'The yellow leaf';
e) Lady Macbeth

2 a) Angus says that there are revolts or rebellions against him
every minute ('minutely'). He adds that those who support him
are only following orders and not out of real 'love'.

b) Macbeth is unafraid and seems buoyed up by the witches'
prophecies. He sees it as the final battle which will 'chair me
ever' or 'dis-seat me now'.

c) He mocks him and his pale appearance calling him a 'cream-
faced loon', 'lily-livered' and 'whey-face', all traits that suggest
the servant is terrified.

3

Point/detail	Evidence	Effect or explanation
1: Macbeth's rule is seen as a disease.	'cannot buckle his distempered cause / Within the belt of rule.' (lines 15–16)	Macbeth's cause is evil, so he himself has lost control, like an illness that can't be kept in.
2: The invading army is seen as the necessary cure to get rid of the disease (Macbeth).	'the medicine of the sickly weal … pour we in our country's purge / Each drop of us.'	Malcolm and the English will drive out ('purge') the infection and make Scotland well again. It hints that every drop of spilled blood will be the medicine that cures the disease.
3: Macbeth is compared to a destructive weed that needs killing off.	'to dew the sovereign flower and drown the weeds'	The blood spilt in battle ('dew') will help Malcolm (the rightful king) 'grow' in strength at the same time destroying Macbeth.

Act V Scenes 4, 5 and 6 [pp. 36–7]

1 a) 3; b) 1: c) 4; d) 2: e) 5; f) 7; g) 6

2 a) The prophecy that Birnan Wood would move to Dunsinane is
made real when Malcolm's army cuts down trees from Birnan
Wood to hide their numbers and then, using the branches and
leaves as camouflage, marches towards Dunsinane. Macduff
reveals he wasn't 'born of woman' (in the usual way) but
'untimely ripped' from her stomach – i.e. by caesarian section.

b) He does not run or try to flee but fights fiercely. He shows some
compassion, initially refusing to fight Macduff as he has already
spilt too much of Macduff's family's blood.

c) It contributes to the reality and brutality of war, also reminding
us of Macbeth's brutal and skilful talents as a fighter/soldier. It
reminds us of other fathers and sons in the play – Macduff
losing his children, but Fleance and Malcolm surviving,
suggesting there is an element of fate in who survives and rises
to power.

3

Point/detail	Evidence	Effect or explanation
1: We witness the one-to-one combat between Macbeth and Macduff.	'Turn, hellhound, turn!' (Act V Scene 6 line 42)	This satisfies our desire to see Macbeth meet his fate and for good to triumph.
2: Shakespeare cleverly reveals how the prophecies have come true, and have 'tricked' Macbeth.	The soldiers cut down Birnan Wood for camouflage. Macduff was not 'born of woman'.	The shock of the news about Birnan Wood creates expectation about Macbeth's downfall. We might expect Macbeth to surrender at Macduff's revelation, but the audience is presented with the dramatic set-piece encounter between villain and nemesis.
3: Shakespeare introduces movement and action which in turn creates excitement.	There are many entrances, exits, 'alarums' and pieces of hand-to-hand combat.	Characters coming onto and then leaving the stage create a sense of momentum; the tension bubbles up to the point of release (Macbeth's death) and the resolution, Malcolm's final speech.

PART THREE: CHARACTERS [pp. 39–46]

Who's who? [p. 39]

1 Top row, left to right: Banquo; Macbeth; Lady Macbeth; Duncan,
King of Scotland.

Bottom row: Macduff; Three witches; Duncan's son and heir to
throne; Seyward

2

Scottish lords or ladies	Scottish children: other sons, daughters, brothers, or sisters	Characters from England who fight against Macbeth	Others?
Ross	Fleance		Old Man
Angus	Macduff's children	Young Seyward	Gentlewoman
Lennox			Seyton
Menteth	Donalbain		English Doctor
Cathness			Scottish Doctor
Unnamed 'Lord'			Hecat
Lady Macduff			Captain (in Duncan's army)
			Messengers
			Murderers
			Servants

King Duncan [p. 40]

1 a) T; b) T; c) T; d) F; e) NEE; f) F; g) T

2 a) Duncan's kingdom is under threat at the start of the play from *Norway and from rebels within his kingdom such as Macdonwald and Cawdor.*

b) Duncan shows himself to be a poor judge of character by *trusting the Thane of Cawdor and believing Macbeth will be satisfied with being made Thane of Cawdor himself.*

c) Macbeth is reluctant to kill Duncan because *he is his host and should be the one protecting him, and because Duncan's virtues will be made to seem even greater once he is dead.*

d) Although Duncan is killed early in the play, he casts a shadow over Macbeth because *he is seen as the rightful king and had chosen his successor; he is seen as divinely chosen.*

e) Duncan is linked to other characters in the play, such as *Malcolm and Donalbain, his sons, and those who remain loyal to his memory such as Macduff.*

Macbeth [p. 41]

1

Macbeth's abilities as a soldier and warrior	1 He is able to defeat the rebels despite the odds being against him.
	2 He fights bravely and skilfully until he is finally killed by Macduff.
His changing feelings of conscience	1 He is reluctant to kill Duncan and suffers ghostly visions after he has ordered the killing of Banquo.
	2 He shows little remorse when he orders the murder of Macduff and his family and his visions seem to stop.
His murderous acts	1 He personally kills Duncan, the two grooms and Seyward's son.
	2 He orders the killings of Banquo and Macduff's family.

2

Evidence	For	Against
Macbeth immediately thinks about how he can overcome the fact that Malcolm is made heir.	✓	
Lady Macbeth makes the plans for Duncan's murder.		✓
Macbeth seems guilty and reluctant to kill the king.		✓
Lady Macbeth has to persuade him to go through with it.		✓
He carries out the killing himself, and kills the servants.	✓	
He organises the murders of Banquo and Macduff's family.	✓	

Lady Macbeth [p. 42]

1 Probable choices: *murderous, powerful, evil, ambitious, cruel, unstable, cunning, guilty*

Possible: *proud, violent*

Not so likely: *feminine, motherly, dignified, gentle, welcoming, desperate*

2 We first meet Lady Macbeth as she is reading a letter from **Macbeth** in Act I Scene 5, which seems to sow the seeds for **Duncan**'s murder. However, she is concerned about whether Macbeth has the the **strength of will/courage** to carry out the plans and she has to question his **manliness** in order to get him to act. When Macbeth falters both after the murder of the king, and at the banquet, she has to invent **excuses** for his behaviour. But, increasingly, he acts without consulting her, preferring her to be '**innocent** of the knowledge'. The stress of maintaining their position and the thought of the murders of Duncan, Banquo and **Lady Macduff** clearly weigh on her mind, and she suffers terrible **guilt**. Eventually, we find out that she has died 'by self and violent hands', according to Malcolm who calls her a '**fiend**-like queen'.

Banquo [p. 43]

1 a) First witch: '**Lesser** than Macbeth, and greater.'

b) Duncan: '**Noble** Banquo, /That hast no less deserved'

c) 'I fear /Thou playedst most **foully** for't'

d) Macbeth: 'There is none but he/Whose being I do **fear**'

e) 'I drink to the general joy o'the whole table,/And to our **dear friend** Banquo, whom we miss.'

2

There is no correct set of answers here: each of these points could be used to suggest Banquo is both ambitious and not ambitious. For example, does he refuse to support Macbeth because he is loyal to Duncan, or because he believes he deserves more than being Macbeth's supporter?

Macduff [p. 44]

1 a) The Porter; b) Macbeth; c) Lennox; d) Lady Macduff; e) Malcolm; f) Macbeth

2 a) Macduff had not come to see Macbeth crowned and had refused to come to the banquet. The apparitions had told Macbeth to 'fear' Macduff, and he'd decided to make doubly sure he couldn't be harmed despite the prophecy promising no one 'born of woman' could injure him.

b) Macduff tells Malcolm it is time to 'hold fast the mortal sword'; in other words, it is time for action, not for sadness and reflection. For Macduff, leaving things even for a minute is not an option as every day 'new widows' are created.

c) Macduff is emotionally broken by the news to begin with and has to ask Ross several times to confirm it is true. It prompts him to vow revenge on Macbeth.

The Witches [p. 45]

1 a) T; b) F; c) NEE; d) T; e) F (it's the apparition)

2 a) The witches' opening scene establishes some important themes in the play such as *appearance versus reality ('foul is fair'), and war or conflict ('battle lost and won'), as well as the general riddling nature of what they say.*

b) The witches' prophecies for Banquo have a riddling quality because *they seem to offer him more and less than Macbeth at the same time. He is 'lesser' and 'greater'; not so happy and 'happier'. He won't be a king, but he will 'get' ('beget') kings.*

c) In Act IV Scene 1, Macbeth believes that the witches have the power to affect the natural world, for example *when he says they can 'untie the winds', make the waves rough, knock down corn and trees.*

ANSWERS

Malcolm, Lady Macduff and Ross [p. 46]

1

Quotation	Malcolm	Lady Macduff	Ross
'This murderous shaft that's shot / Hath not yet lighted'	✓		
'By the clock 'tis day, / And yet dark night strangles the travelling lamp'			✓
'I take my leave of you; / Shall not be long but I'll be here again'			✓
'I have done no harm.'		✓	
'Macbeth / Is ripe for shaking.'	✓		

2 a) Macbeth and his brother believe that the violence hasn't ended and they could be next to be murdered. They don't trust people at Macbeth's castle.

b) Ross tells Macbeth that Duncan knows of his success in battle and that as a reward he has made him Thane of Cawdor. He also outlines the reasons for this – Cawdor being a traitor.

c) Lady Macduff is upset because her husband has left without giving any reason for his actions. She says it must be because he doesn't love her or the children as they are defenceless.

PART FOUR: THEMES, CONTEXTS AND SETTINGS [pp. 48–55]

Themes [pp. 48–51]

1 Likely answers: *Ambition Witchcraft The supernatural Fate Revenge Kingship Evil Guilt Betrayal Appearance/reality Conflict/war*

Possible answers: *Greed Regret Fatherhood*

Less likely answers: *Motherhood Love Religion Journeys Childhood*

2 a) 'Peace! The charm's wound up.'

Theme: the supernatural
Speakers: The three witches

b) 'Your children shall be kings.'

Themes: ambition, kingship, fate
Speaker: Macbeth

c) 'Come, thick night / And pall thee in the dunnest smoke of hell'

Themes: evil, the supernatural, witchcraft
Speaker: Lady Macbeth

d) 'art thou but / A dagger of the mind, a false creation, / Proceeding from the heat-oppressèd brain?'

Themes: the supernatural, evil, guilt, ambition
Speaker: Macbeth

e) 'Front to front / Bring thou this fiend of Scotland and myself. / Within my sword's length set him'

Themes: revenge, fate
Speaker: Macduff

f) 'Of all men else I have avoided thee. / ... my soul is too much charged / With blood of thine already.'

Themes: guilt, revenge, fate
Speaker: Macbeth

3 a) The mention of Macbeth's name in the witches' chanting links him to them from the start. It also links witchcraft to themes such as appearance and reality and conflict in the form of war.

b) Before Macbeth's arrival back at the castle, Lady Macbeth asks devilish spirits to take over her body and remove any femininity so that she has the strength of mind to act.

4 a) Macbeth sees the dagger that seems to be leading him to Duncan's rooms in Act II Scene 2.

b) Macbeth sees the ghost of Banquo in Act III Scene 4.

c) Lady Macbeth 'sees' spots of blood on her hands when she is sleepwalking in Act V Scene 1.

5 a) Macbeth is told he is Thane of Cawdor, yet he is in fact Thane of Glamis:

Comes true because: The Thane of Cawdor is captured and shown to be a traitor. He is executed and his title given to Macbeth as a reward for his valour in battle.

b) Macbeth is told he is safe until Birnan Wood moves to Dunsinane (his castle):

Comes true because: Malcolm's army cuts down branches from the wood to disguise their numbers, and then, camouflaged in this way, marches towards Dunsinane hill near Macbeth's castle.

c) Macbeth is told he cannot be harmed by anyone 'of woman born'.

Comes true because: Macduff was 'untimely ripped' from his mother's stomach, meaning he was born by caesarian section rather than in the 'conventional' way.

6 We find out early in the play that the Thane of **Cawdor** has betrayed Duncan. Duncan admits that he finds it difficult to 'find the **mind's** construction in the face', in other words to read people's thoughts. Both Lady Macbeth and Macbeth betray Duncan by welcoming him to **their castle** and pretending to be kind hosts, and then murdering him. But the betrayal is also of the innocent **servants/grooms** who are also killed. Macbeth might feel that **Banquo** betrays him when he refuses to commit to supporting him, but the real betrayal is when he orders the murders of Banquo and his son, **Fleance**. Perhaps the biggest betrayal in the play is not of one person, but of a country – **Scotland**. It is said that it '**weeps**' and 'bleeds' under Macbeth's rule.

8

Point/detail	Evidence	Effect or explanation
1: *Macbeth sees his own future success in what the witches have said.*	Macbeth: 'The greatest is behind' (line 116)	*The witches have proved correct on one promise, so the next step is now in sight.*
2: *Banquo is less trusting of the witches.*	'To win us to our harm / The instruments of darkness tell us truths.' (lines 122–3)	*Banquo sees that evil often uses subtle methods to 'win' people, for example delivering rewards but with what is owed in return being too costly.*
3: *The supernatural can be frightening and both hide and reveal the truth.*	'Horrible sight! Now I see 'tis true, / For the blood-boltered Banquo smiles upon me, / And points at them for his.' (Act IV Scene 1 lines 121–3)	*Macbeth is appalled by the visions of the kings, but is forced to face the truth that they are Banquo's heirs.*

Contexts [pp. 52–3]

1 a) Holinshed; b) *Joe Macbeth*; c) James I; d) *Demonology*;
e) The Gunpowder Plot; f) The King was Shakespeare's patron;
g) The succession; h) Divine Right of Kings

2 a) The play starts with thunder and lightning which suggests conflict; the witches mention the 'battle lost and won' but we don't know who is fighting or who has been victorious. The second scene shows how close the rebels were to winning the battle until Macbeth and Banquo's efforts.

b) Malcolm regains the crown passed on to him by his father, the rightful king. Macbeth and Lady Macbeth, the usurpers, are dead.

c) The fact that Macbeth doesn't have any outside supporters makes his crime very personal. Making Lady Macbeth his partner in crime is also unusual as women weren't usually shown in this way.

3

	Lady Macbeth	Lady Macduff
a) Her husband – what is he like?	Macbeth seems to shift from uncertainty to murder; he is first presented as loyal then as a murdering traitor. He seems close to her at start.	Macduff seems consistent throughout in opposing Macbeth. However, he leaves his family unguarded.
b) Her children (if any)	She has no children though she refers to being a mother.	She has children, and seems very caring.
c) Her actions	She plans Duncan's murder and encourages Macbeth to become king.	She looks after her children, and is essentially passive and defenceless.
d) How she dies	By her own hand (probably)	Murdered by Macbeth's hired killers

Settings [pp. 54–5]

1 Inverness, Macbeth's castle – where Duncan and Banquo are murdered

Dunsinane, Macbeth's fortress – where he dies fighting Macduff, and where Lady Macbeth dies too

Birnan Wood – where the soldiers of Malcolm's army cut down trees to disguise themselves

The heath – where the witches meet Macbeth and Banquo

England, King Edward's palace – where Malcolm meets Macduff and plans invasion

2 a) Act I Scene 1

Takes place outside – 'Thunder and lightning'.

It involves the three witches.

Its setting is important because it establishes stormy, violent weather and the presence of witchcraft and 'evil' things.

b) Act III Scene 3

Takes place outside Macbeth's castle, at night time.

It involves Banquo, Fleance and the three murderers.

Its setting is important because the darkness, the putting out of the light and the proximity to the castle all stress the power of evil and Macbeth's hand in it.

c) Act III Scene 4

Takes place at Macbeth's castle.

It involves 'King and Queen' Macbeth, important lords, the ghost of Banquo, but *not* Macduff.

Its setting is important because the banquet is supposed to be the highpoint of the Macbeths' power, a time when they can enjoy their position. The ghost ruins this feast of celebration, indicating that their reign will not be trouble-free.

3

Significant arrivals	Macbeth, after the battle; Duncan and his entourage; Macduff and other lords
Murders	Duncan, the two grooms, Banquo
Visions/ghosts	Bloody dagger; Banquo's ghost
Departures	Macduff for Fife; Malcolm and Donalbain to escape

PART FIVE: FORM, STRUCTURE AND LANGUAGE [pp. 57–62]

Form [p. 57]

1 a) Five

2 'Thunder and lightning. Enter three Witches': Act I Scene 1

'Enter a Porter. Knocking within': Act II Scene 3

'Banquet prepared. Enter Macbeth, Lady Macbeth, Ross, Lennox, Lords, and Attendants': Act III Scene 4

3 b) Rhyming couplets

4 Iambic **pentameter** is the dominant form in Shakespeare's verse. It contains **five** iambic feet, each one made up of two **syllables**. The second is always **stressed**.

5 The Porter speaks in prose at the start of Act II Scene 3. It is often used for lighter, more informal speech. It is also sometimes used by characters of lower social status, like servants.

6 The witches' style of speech is different because they often speak in very rhythmic forms, using rhyming couplets, spells, chants, etc. They also say some lines together, speaking with one voice.

Structure [pp. 58–9]

1 a) F; b) T; c) T; d) F; e) F (only one in Act III – Banquo)

2

The Porter's speech before he opens the gate	4
Lady Macbeth's 'milk of human kindness' speech while waiting for Macbeth	1
Macbeth's speech weighing up the pros and cons of killing Duncan	2
Macbeth's speech in which he reflects about Banquo being a threat to him	5
Macbeth's 'dagger' speech as he is on his way to murder Duncan	3

ANSWERS

3

Point/detail	Evidence	Effect or explanation
1: Malcolm explains the surprising manner of how the traitor Cawdor faced his execution.	'he ... set forth / A deep repentance.' (lines 7–8)	This establishes the theme of a traitor's regret, and introduces the idea of people being difficult to 'read'.
2: Duncan says it is impossible to judge people from how they look.	'There's no art / To find the mind's construction in the face.'	Duncan seems to accept that he has taken people at face value which is ironic given that he then walks into the trap set by Macbeth and his wife by inviting himself to their castle.
3: Macbeth pledges loyalty to Duncan, his family and followers.	'our duties / Are to your throne and state, children and servants'	This is a further irony as his 'duty' is that he will take the throne and state by killing Duncan, force Malcolm and Donalbain to flee, and lay the blame on the servants by murdering them.

Language [pp. 60–2]

1 a) robes; b) naked; c) pictures; d) scorpions; e) grave

2

image of arrow shot by murderers of Duncan

'This murderous shaft that's shot
Hath not yet lighted; and our safest way
Is to avoid the aim.'

it hasn't yet fallen to earth so can still injure others

it's best to get out of sight of the archer

3 a) SLEEP

Act II Scene 2: After Duncan's murder

Act V Scene 1: Lady Macbeth sleepwalking

In Act II Scene 2 sleep is associated with peace and death. Duncan and the grooms are asleep when murdered, so when Macbeth says he 'does murder sleep' it is literally true, as he has both stopped them sleeping properly and sent them to sleep forever.

However, he also says, 'Macbeth shall sleep no more', which seems to refer to being at peace – that he won't be able to sleep because of his feelings of guilt for what he's done. This links to Act V Scene 1 when we see Lady Macbeth's sleep visibly destroyed by what she has done. The Doctor calls it a 'great perturbation in nature'.

b) BLOOD

Act II Scene 2: After Duncan's murder

Act III Scene 4: The banquet scene

Macbeth is appalled by the sight of the king's blood on his hands. He says his hands, 'pluck out mine eyes!' and that no amount of water, not even 'great Neptune's ocean' will remove it, a foretaste of Lady Macbeth's words in Act V Scene 1. In Act III Scene 4, Macbeth says, 'Blood will have blood', which could refer to 'family blood' as in who is heir to the throne, but also the idea that spilling blood violently will 'have' consequences for the killer.

c) WEATHER AND NATURE

Act I Scene 1

Act II Scene 4

In the opening scene the thunder and lightning seems to reflect heaven's anger or nature being shaken up by the actions on earth – the battle. The scene ends with a reference to 'fog and filthy air'; no one can see through it, ideal conditions for murder and betrayal. In Act II Scene 4 the Old Man and Ross describe the strangeness of the weather – it is so dark that even though it is day, the darkness 'strangles the travelling lamp' – a perfect metaphor for the murderous act of the night before.

4

Point/detail	Evidence	Effect or explanation
1: Antithesis is used to convey the idea that characters can be deceptive.	'Fair is foul, and foul is fair.' (Act I Scene 1 line 9)	Characters who seem to be trustworthy – Cawdor, Macbeth and Lady Macbeth – turn out not to be so.
2: Nature imagery is used to show the world turned upside down.	'A falcon towering in her pride of place, / Was by a mousing owl hawked at and killed.'	This symbolically represents what has happened in real life: the falcon (i.e. Duncan), the more powerful bird, is killed by the normally weaker bird, the owl (Macbeth).
3: Evil and innocence are contrasted in speeches such as Lady Macbeth's when calling on the powers of darkness.	'take my milk for gall, you murdering ministers'	Lady Macbeth asks that milk from her breasts, associated with love and nourishment, be transformed into poison.

PART SIX: PROGRESS BOOSTER

Writing skills [pp. 64–5]

2 Student A: Mid

Clear point that provides evidence in the form of a quotation; explanation isn't developed or explained in more detail.

Student B: Higher

Clear point with appropriate quotation for evidence; specific comment on particular word from the quotation, mentioning it is an adjective and explaining its effect; further explanation and link to related point (Banquo asking for a 'sword').

4, 5 and **6**

*Shakespeare **suggests** that Macbeth is shocked by Lady Macbeth's ruthless ambition when he says, 'Bring forth men-children only!' This **indicates** that Lady Macbeth is more likely to produce men, traditionally more aggressive than girls. It also **implies** that she is not a natural mother.*

Making inferences and interpretations [p. 66]

1 _In Act II Scene 4, Macbeth tells Lady Macbeth that he will do anything for 'mine own good', in other words do anything to keep himself safe._ [simple point]

He also says that because he is in 'blood stepped in so far … returning were as tedious as go o'er'. This is a metaphor which tells us that he might as well continue with violent acts as he has already committed so many. [development of first point]

It also implies that he has become dehumanised; from now on he seems to act mechanically, as if racing towards his fate as there can be no turning back. [inference]

2 b) _he has not behaved well or played his role in life as he should have done_

Writing about context [p. 67]

1 b) It makes the link between the way Malcolm is presented and ideas of kingship in Shakespeare's time.

2 c) _people's concerns at the time when rational or scientific explanations for natural disasters, illnesses and death were not available, and belief in demons or witches was quite widespread._

Structure and linking of paragraphs [pp. 68–9]

1 _Shakespeare presents Duncan as a saintly, well-respected king._ [topic sentence]

Even Macbeth when thinking about murdering him is forced to accept that, 'his virtues / Will plead like angels' …

The use of the nouns 'virtues' and 'angels' link Duncan to divine or heavenly character traits [explanation of words], _and therefore make Macbeth's potential murder of him all the more sinful._

2 Possible answer:

Shakespeare presents Lady Macbeth in this scene as feeling terrible guilt about her part in the murders. We see this when she is sleepwalking and asks, 'What, will these hands ne'er be clean?' (Act V Scene 1 line 42). The phrase 'ne'er be clean' has a metaphorical meaning, suggesting that the murders have left an emotional stain on her which cannot be removed, whatever she does.

3 _Shakespeare presents Lady Macduff as an isolated, innocent mother who acts as a contrast to Lady Macbeth. She is initially shown as independent of thought, questioning her husband's motives, saying his 'flight was madness' and even telling her son, only partly in jest, that his father was a 'traitor.' However, later in the scene it is her vulnerability that is most powerful. When the messenger appears, her simple question, 'Whither should I fly?' implies she has nowhere to go, and nowhere to turn._

4 Possible answer:

Shakespeare presents us with a sympathetic portrayal of Lady Macduff. When the messenger appears and warns her about danger, he says, 'Hence with your little ones' which tells us that the children are in Macbeth's sights. It reminds us of the fragile nature of life, and her simple statement, 'I have done no harm' emphasises her innocence. Eventually, the murderers come in and accuse her husband of treason. Her innocence is highlighted by our last sight of her, running from the stage, about to be murdered.

Spelling, punctuation and grammar [pp. 70–1]

3 _At the end of Act I, the tension builds dramatically as Macbeth claims he has 'no spur' for killing Duncan. In his dialogue with Lady Macbeth it is clear he is uncertain whether to proceed with the murder and it is only when his wife condemns him for not being a man, that he rises to the challenge. By the time the curtain falls, Shakespeare ensures that the audience knows that Macbeth is 'settled' on committing this 'terrible feat'._

4 _When **Shakespeare** refers to the witches as the **'weird sisters'** he is suggesting that they form a close blood bond, as if they were one entity rather than three separate people. **This** gives their speech extra power, almost as if each time they speak it could be one voice. **For example**, in **Act I Scene 1** we see **Shakespeare's** decision to separate their three lines 'I come, Grey-Malkin', 'Paddock calls', and 'Anon!' (line 9) but rhythmically allow it to be structured as if a single line of speech._

5 Student B

6 _Shakespeare decides to make Ross the character who is present with Lady Macduff as Act 4 Scene 2 opens. He keeps his views to himself and refuses to answer her questions directly, and says, 'I dare not speak much further', which implies he knows what is about to happen._

Decoding questions [p. 72]

1 Explain how Shakespeare explores Lady Macbeth's conscience:

In this extract

In the play as a whole

Sample answers [pp. 74–5]

1	Student A	1 – mid level
	Student B	2 – lower level
3	Student A	2 – mid level
	Student B	1 – higher level